SHEPHERD'S NOTES

SHEPHERD'S NOTES

When you need a guide through the Scriptures

Ruth, Esther

BROADMAN
&HOLMAN
PUBLISHERS

Nashville, Tennessee

© 1998

by Broadman & Holman Publishers

Nashville, Tennessee

All rights reserved

Printed in the United States of America

0–8054–9057–4

Dewey Decimal Classification: 222.35

Subject Heading: BIBLE. O.T. RUTH

Library of Congress Card Catalog Number: 97–32781

Library of Congress Cataloging-in-Publication Data

Ruth, Esther / Robert Lintzenich, editor

      p. cm. — (Shepherd's notes)

    Includes bibliographical references.

    ISBN 0–8054–9057–4

    1. Bible. O.T. Ruth—Study and teaching. 2. Bible. O.T. Esther—Study and
teaching. I. Lintzenich, Robert. II. Series
    BS1315.5.R88   1998
    222'.3507—dc21

                    97–32781
                      CIP

1 2 3 4 5 6   03 02 01 00 99 98

CONTENTS

FOREWORD

Dear Reader:

Shepherd's Notes are designed to give you a quick, step-by-step overview of every book of the Bible. They are not meant to be substitutes for the biblical text; rather, they are study guides intended to help you explore the wisdom of Scripture in personal or group study and to apply that wisdom successfully in your own life.

Shepherd's Notes guide you through the main themes of each book of the Bible and illuminate fascinating details through appropriate commentary and reference notes. Historical and cultural background information brings the Bible into sharper focus.

Six different icons, used throughout the series, call your attention to historical-cultural information, Old Testament and New Testament references, word pictures, unit summaries, and personal application for everyday life.

Whether you are a novice or a veteran at Bible study, I believe you will find *Shepherd's Notes* a resource that will take you to a new level in your mining and applying the riches of Scripture.

In Him,

David R. Shepherd
Editor-in-Chief

DESIGNED FOR THE BUSY USER

Shepherd's Notes for Ruth and Esther is designed to provide an easy-to-use tool for getting a quick handle on these significant Bible books, important features, and for gaining an understanding of their messages. Information available in more difficult-to-use reference works has been incorporated into the *Shepherd's Notes* format. This brings you the benefits of many advanced and expensive works packed into one small volume.

Shepherd's Notes are for laymen, pastors, teachers, small-group leaders and participants, as well as the classroom student. Enrich your personal study or quiet time. Shorten your class or small-group preparation time as you gain valuable insights into the truths of God's Word that you can pass along to your students or group members.

DESIGNED FOR QUICK ACCESS

Bible students with time constraints will especially appreciate the timesaving features built into the *Shepherd's Notes*. All features are intended to aid a quick and concise encounter with the heart of the messages of Ruth and Esther.

Concise Commentary. The books of Ruth and Esther are filled with characters, subplots, details, and events. Short sections provide quick "snapshots" of the narrative and themes of these books, highlighting important points and other information.

Outlined Text. Comprehensive outlines cover the entire texts of Ruth and Esther. This is a valuable feature for following each narrative's flow, allowing for a quick, easy way to locate a particular passage.

Shepherd's Notes. These summary statements or capsule thoughts appear at the close of every key section of the narratives. While functioning in part as a quick summary, they also deliver the essence of the message presented in the sections which they cover.

Icons. Various icons in the margin highlight recurring themes in the books of Ruth and Esther, aiding in selective searching or tracing of those themes.

Sidebars and Charts. These specially selected features provide additional background information to your study or preparation. Charts offer a quick overview of important subjects. Sidebars include definitions as well as cultural, historical, and biblical insights.

Maps. These are placed at appropriate places in the book to aid your understanding and study of a text or passage.

Questions to Guide Your Study. These thought-provoking questions and discussion starters are designed to encourage interaction with the truth and principles of God's Word.

DESIGNED TO WORK FOR YOU

Personal Study. Using *Shepherd's Notes* with a passage of Scripture can enlighten your study and take it to a new level. At your fingertips is information that would require searching several volumes to find. In addition, many points of application occur throughout the volume, contributing to personal growth.

Teaching. Outlines frame the texts of Ruth and Esther, providing a logical presentation of their messages. Capsule thoughts designated as "Shepherd's Notes" provide summary statements for presenting the essence of key points and events. Application icons point out personal application of the messages of these books. Historical Context icons indicate where cultural and historical background information is supplied.

Group Study. *Shepherd's Notes* can be an excellent companion volume to use for gaining a quick but accurate understanding of the messages of Ruth and Esther. Each group member can benefit by having his or her own copy. The *Notes'* format accommodates the study of themes throughout Ruth and Esther. Leaders may use its flexible features to prepare for group sessions or use them during group sessions. Questions to guide your study can spark discussion of Ruth and Esther's key points and truths to be discovered in these delightful books.

LIST OF MARGIN ICONS USED IN RUTH AND ESTHER

 Shepherd's Notes. Placed at the end of each section, a capsule statement provides the reader with the essence of the message of that section.

 Old Testament Reference. Used when the writer refers to Old Testament passages or when Old Testament passages illuminate a text.

 New Testament Reference. Used when the writer refers to New Testament passages that are related to or have a bearing on the passage's understanding or interpretation.

 Historical Background. To indicate historical, cultural, geographical, or biographical information that sheds light on the understanding or interpretation of a passage.

 Personal Application. Used when the text provides a personal or universal application of truth.

 Word Picture. Indicates that the meaning of a specific word or phrase is illustrated so as to shed light on it.

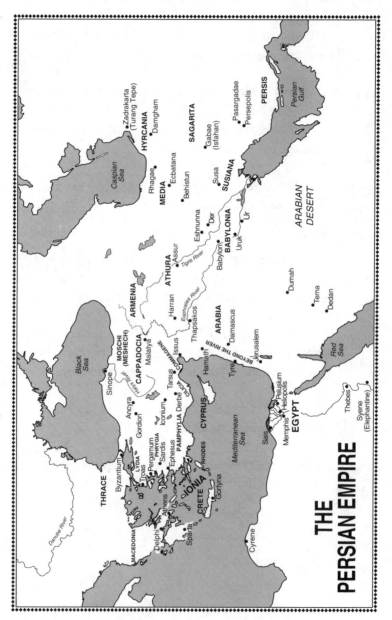

Taken from Jay A. Thompson, *Chronicles,* vol. 9, New American Commentary (Nashville, Tenn.: Broadman & Holman Publishers), p. 20.

INTRODUCTION

Only two books in the Bible are named after women—the books of Ruth and Esther. Both books offer beautiful stories, literally masterpieces of narrative. While the books are distinct from each other in some ways, the striking similarities between Ruth and Esther make it profitable to read these stories back to back, observing the impact that two women had on the Jewish people.

HISTORICAL SETTING

The stories of Ruth and Esther took place in different time periods, with about seven hundred years between them. Ruth is set in the time of the judges; Esther, in the postexilic period. The genealogy in the book of Ruth (Ruth 4:18–22) shows a family line of mother, son, grandson, great-grandson (Ruth, Obed, Jesse, David). Counting backward from King David's reign would place Ruth at approximately 1200 B.C. Esther is set during the reign of Persia's King Xerxes (486–465 B.C.). Although taking place in different times, Ruth and Esther speak to some of the same issues.

A FOREIGN LAND

One theme found in both books is foreignness. Ruth was a woman from Moab who left her homeland to reside in Bethlehem of Judah with her mother-in-law. Esther was a Jewish woman living in the city of Susa, one of four capital cities of the Persian Empire. Her people had been exiled from Judah in 597 B.C., and she had lived all of her life in a foreign land. For both women, their foreignness had a significant effect upon the development of their stories.

The Family Covenant

The Old Testament family was close-knit, and family loyalty was very strong. The stories of Ruth and Esther display the bonding of family relationships based on the idea of covenant. Two different families lived during two different time periods: Ruth and Naomi in Bethlehem; Esther and Mordecai in Susa of Persia. Yet the interactions of the people in both of these families demonstrate family covenants that were caring and personal.

DIVINE PROVIDENCE

Another common theme of Ruth and Esther is even similar in the manner of presentation. While both books reveal the working of God in the lives of His people, both present divine activity indirectly. God worked, but He worked behind the scenes. His name was mentioned by the characters of Ruth's story as they blessed one another, but only twice does the narrator describe the Lord as performing some action. In Esther's story, God's name is not mentioned at all. Despite these apparent absences, the reader is aware of God's presence as He delivered Naomi and Ruth from the certain poverty of widowhood and Esther's Jewish people from annihilation.

God's presence is assumed throughout these stories. While the events of the stories may appear to be coincidences and in some cases to have little significance, God was directing the action. God was controlling the scenes and moving toward a greater goal. But He did not work through miracles or displays of power; He worked through people of unpretentious backgrounds as they proved faithful to Him.

LITERARY CRAFTSMANSHIP

Ruth and Esther are not just good stories; both are carefully crafted pieces of literature. A symmetrical structure can be outlined for these stories. Both stories contain a key turning point and finish with a happy ending.

Tension builds in Ruth with the main characters facing widowhood and a struggle to support themselves. At the approximate midpoint of the story, the plot turns, as Naomi realizes that Boaz is one of her kinsman-redeemers. Hope is

Loyal to the Lord

God's covenant with Israel was not limited to a particular time period nor to a specific geographical region. It was a covenant pointed to all the earth for all ages. Ruth, a Moabitess, left Moab's gods and became integrated into Israel's family of faith. Hundreds of years later, Esther, in the land of Persia, learned that to be loyal to Israel's covenant God meant faithfully serving His people.

renewed not only for Naomi, but for the reader as well.

In Esther, tension and suspense build as they do in Ruth. Only the forces that threaten are different. Instead of the natural calamities of famine and poverty, the main characters faced a human enemy who would destroy them along with all their people. As in Ruth, a turning point occurs midway through the story. To pass a sleepless night, the king listened to a reading of the royal chronicles (Esther 6:1). What he heard that night changed the story's course.

THE FIVE SCROLLS

In the Greek and English versions of the Bible, Ruth and Esther are part of the collection called the historical books. The books of Joshua, Judges, Samuel, Kings, Chronicles, Ezra, and Nehemiah trace the history of Israel from the conquest of Canaan to the Jews' return to Jerusalem after the Exile. The books of Ruth and Esther are placed according to their respective historical contexts, with Ruth following the book of Judges and Esther following Ezra and Nehemiah (which recount events of the Persian period).

In the Hebrew arrangement of the Old Testament, Esther and Ruth are two of the five *Megilloth* (meaning "rolls" or "scrolls"). Each of the five scrolls was read annually at a festival: Song of Songs at Passover; Ruth at Pentecost; Lamentations on the ninth of Ab; Ecclesiastes at the Feast of Tabernacles; and Esther at Purim.

Traditionally then, the stories of Ruth and Esther are read by Jews each year. Ruth is read at the harvest festival—the Feast of Weeks (also known as Pentecost). Esther, naturally, is read annually on Adar 14 and 15, at the Feast of Purim. How appropriate it is to read these two books at festivals, for both call for celebration of God's deliverance. How appropriate to read together two books with so many similarities in their messages and in their manner of presentation.

These two books are both named for women and have women as their main characters—Ruth and Esther. Furthermore, when Israel reads Scripture at the festivals, two of the five books read annually are these stories whose leading characters are females.

The book of Ruth is named for its heroine, whose devotion to God and love for family has endeared her to generations of readers. Ruth's story tells how God graciously rewarded the faithfulness of the widows Ruth and Naomi by delivering them through their kinsman-redeemer Boaz.

The interaction of Boaz and Ruth shows the ways of God in one unique family situation, but this one family reveals much about Israelite family customs, marriage patterns, and obligations. The plot revolves around the custom of levirate marriage as a family obligation at work.

AUTHOR

The authorship of Ruth is unknown. A late Jewish tradition ascribes the book to the prophet Samuel. Samuel, however, died before David became king, making it less likely that he would write of Ruth's son, Obed, being David's grandfather (4:17, 22).

Whoever authored Ruth apparently did so several years after the time at which the events themselves occurred. The story took place during the time of the judges (about 1200 B.C.), but the author introduced his story with a reference back to that time period (1:1). It was also necessary for the author to explain the customs of Ruth's time, since his readers were no longer familiar with them (4:7).

DATE OF WRITING

The date of composition is likewise unknown, but it has been estimated to be either the early monarchy (about 950 B.C.) or the postexilic period (about 450 B.C.). The question of date is affected by how one relates the story to the genealogy of David, which ends the book (4:18–22).

It is unusual for a book to end with a genealogy, and some scholars believe the story originally had no connection with David. An editor, writing during the postexilic period, could have borrowed the genealogy from 1 Chronicles 2:4–15 and added it as an appendix to the story.

Other scholars, though, think it unlikely that David would have been linked to a Moabite ancestress unless he was in fact her descendant. The genealogies in Ruth and Chronicles could have come from a common Temple source, and one writer, writing about 950 B.C., could have written the story of Ruth presupposing the genealogy.

AUDIENCE

In determining the intended audience for this book, the options are almost the same as those for dating Ruth. Scholars are divided about whether the story fits better with the concerns of people during the monarchy or with those of the postexilic exiles.

The genealogy at the end of the story speaks to political concerns of the time of the monarchy. By providing the details of David's family background, the story served to legitimize

Ruth and Judges

The book of Judges reflects Israel's "dark days." Repeatedly, the Israelites disregarded their covenant obligations by doing as they "saw fit" (Judg. 21:25). In the absence of godly leadership, moral decay set in. There was even a decline in the spiritual condition of the judges themselves as each cycle of the judges passed. For this period of disobedience, the book of Ruth offered encouragement. In such a time of "darkness," Naomi, Ruth, and Boaz stood out as examples of true faithfulness.

No King

Judges shows what happened to Israel when there was no godly king to lead them. The book closes with the author's assessment of the period: "In those days Israel had no king" (Judg. 21:25). The book of Ruth closes with an answer to the dilemma in Judges. Through the genealogy of David (Ruth 4:18–22), the author showed that God was quietly working through an unexpected channel—a Moabite woman—to provide the needed king. David became a role model for Israel's kings and left a legacy never to be forgotten.

David as king on Saul's throne. It also provided a transition from the patriarchs to David's reign by tracing the lineage of Boaz from Perez, the son of Judah, down to King David. For many Israelites the most important word of the book was the last—David.

In a social context, the book of Ruth speaks against the postexilic particularism visible in the books of Ezra and Nehemiah. Ruth, a native of Moab, was accepted into Israel's genealogical mainstream, demonstrating that inclusion into the people of God is not predicated on birth alone.

PURPOSE

Why was the story of Ruth written? The question could have several answers because many messages cross and merge throughout the story. One prominent concern would be to preserve Israelite customs and laws—in this case, the levirate marriage, the kinsman-redeemer, and the inheritance of property. Another concern would be to support the Davidic monarchy, showing how God would bring peace and rest to Israel through the house of David.

The purpose for the writing of Ruth might be found in the main characters of the story. Although Ruth was a Moabitess, she was blessed by God. The story thus countered nationalism with a message of universal acceptance; the worship of God was not exclusively the prerogative of Israel.

Yet another possible reason for reading (and maybe writing) Ruth is to promote specific virtues. By their faithfulness, integrity, and love, the characters themselves mirror the character of God. They serve as reminders that the lives of godly people are a powerful witness to God's self-sacrificing love.

STRUCTURE AND CONTENT

The book of Ruth is an example of good story-telling. Ruth is a self-contained story and is not dependent on other Old Testament narratives for its continuity. The plot moves through a series of four scenes or episodes with different comments by the narrator.

All of the episodes center on faithfulness, both human and divine. The first section (chap. 1) moves from Bethlehem to Moab and back, telling why Naomi was in Moab and of her plight following the deaths of her husband and sons. Important, though, is Ruth's faithfulness as she chose to remain with Naomi.

As the scene changes in the second section (chap. 2), Ruth faced a challenge of faithfulness. Life as a Moabite widow in Bethlehem was not easy, but help arrived as Ruth met Boaz while gleaning grain in his field during the harvest.

In the third section (chap. 3), the plot develops quickly, taking place at a threshing floor near Bethlehem. Ruth made a claim for faithfulness, asking Boaz to be faithful to an Israelite custom concerning childless widows. The story appears to climax when he agreed to fulfill the role of the kinsman-redeemer.

All of the problems and tensions in the story do not come to a final resolution until the fourth section (chap. 4). Boaz met at the town gate with another kinsman to settle matters of property and of Ruth. The removal of the last obstacle cleared the way for a happy ending, as the whole community broke into praise and blessing.

Moab and Israel

Since they were neighbors, the history of the Moabites was intertwined with that of Israel. Moreover, the Israelites regarded the Moabites, who were descended from Abraham's nephew Lot (Gen. 19:30–38), as close relatives. Relations between Israelites and Moabites during the time of the judges varied from peaceful interchange to conflict. While the story of Ruth illustrates peaceful relations, the episode of Ehud and Eglon (Judg. 3:12–30) is an example of early conflict.

LITERARY STYLE

Ruth is a finely crafted historical short story. The literary artistry of the author entertains the reader by highlighting the element of suspense. Transitions at the end of each of the first three episodes (1:22; 2:23; 3:18) keep the plot moving forward. At many points along the way the reader suspects that the outcome will be good, especially so at the turning point of the story when Naomi realized the hope of a kinsman-redeemer (2:20).

THEOLOGY

The story of Ruth reflects a belief in God's lordship in history, but it equally emphasizes the significant role of human actions and decisions. God sovereignly achieves His purposes through the faithfulness of His people.

God acts in the story, although almost imperceptibly. The book speaks about God indirectly through the prayers and blessing of the story's characters. What does become clear is that God's will is sometimes accomplished by common people with uncommon faith. The book of Ruth does not tell of miracles or revelations. Rather, God is present as simple people go about their everyday affairs.

Above all, Ruth is a story of faithfulness. God was faithful in preserving Elimelech's family line, which—in God's time—led to King David and ultimately to Jesus. Yet God often demonstrates His faithfulness through the faithful actions of His people. Naomi was faithful to Ruth, always concerned about Ruth's future welfare. Ruth was faithful to Naomi, working the fields to provide for her.

We should be reminded by Ruth's story that our own faithfulness may play a part in the fulfillment of God's promises. Ruth was faithful to her deceased husband Mahlon in her willingness to marry into his family. Boaz was faithful to Ruth in fulfilling the role of kinsman-redeemer. Without their individual acts of faithfulness, the family line of the Messiah would have been broken.

THE MEANING OF RUTH FOR TODAY

Our experience of God today may be very similar to the experiences related in the book of Ruth. In Ruth, God worked behind the scenes in the lives of ordinary people, turning apparent tragedy into joy and peace.

These common, everyday people, however, challenge us today to match their extraordinary examples of faithfulness and selflessness. The contrast between this book's characters, who are righteous in their relations with each other, and the characters of the book of Judges, who "did as they saw fit" (Judg. 21:25), should instruct our own personal relationships.

One message of the book causes us to view our own lives through the story line. God is concerned not only for the welfare of one family—Naomi and Ruth——but for the welfare of all His people. All who would be blessed by Ruth's descendant, Jesus Christ, can see themselves as participants in the story's happy ending. The participation of Ruth, the Moabitess, in the fulfillment of God's promises indicates that God's salvation is for people of all nationalities.

God's activity in the story of Ruth is assumed rather than announced. The only passages where the story specifically says that God acted on behalf of His people are His "providing food" (Ruth 1:6) and enabling Ruth to conceive (Ruth 4:13). Just as God had caused the land to grow, He would bless the house of Elimelech through Ruth's womb.

The first section of the book of Ruth (1:1–22) introduces the story's heroine by focusing on her choice to be faithful. Ruth dramatically exhibited faithfulness to her mother-in-law, being willing to become one with Naomi's people, Naomi's land, and Naomi's God.

TRIAL IN JUDAH; TRAGEDY IN MOAB (1:1–5)

Naomi's story begins with trial but progresses to tragedy. To escape a trial of famine, her family departed from their home in Bethlehem of Judah, moving to the country of Moab. Yet in Moab Naomi was forced to face tragedy when death came to her family.

Driven by Famine to Moab (1:1–2)

The story transpires at a specific time. "The days when the judges ruled" (1:1) were a dark time in Israel's history, for the people had no king and everyone "did as he saw fit" (Judg. 21:25). This turbulent time was to become even more difficult for the story's main characters.

"Bethlehem"

The name *Bethlehem* means "house of bread," but famine had made the town a house of scarcity.

Naomi's family are described as "Ephrathites from Bethlehem" (1:2). The town of Ephrath was part of Judah's tribal territory, and it is often identified with Bethlehem (Gen. 35:19; 48:7). This particular Ephrathite family included Naomi's husband, Elimelech, and her sons, Mahlon and Kilion.

The food crisis caused Elimelech to leave this area in search of a land where he might provide for his wife, Naomi, and their two sons. The agrarian world of Moab, east of the Dead Sea, held the promise of plenty. Elimelech's desire to care for his family was natural, and his flight to

Moab reminds us of Abraham's journey to Egypt for the same reason (Gen. 12:10).

Ruth's Cast of Characters

CHARACTER	DESCRIPTION	SCRIPTURE
Elimelech	An Ephrathite man from Bethlehem in Judah; the husband of Naomi	Ruth 1:1–2
Naomi	The wife of Elimelech and mother of Mahlon and Kilion	Ruth 1:2
Mahlon	The son of Elimelech and Naomi; the husband of Ruth	Ruth 1:2,4; 4:10
Kilion	The son of Elimelech and Naomi; the husband of Orpah	Ruth 1:2, 4
Ruth	A Moabite woman; the wife of Mahlon and daughter-in-law of Naomi	Ruth 1:4, 22
Orpah	A Moabite woman; the wife of Kilion and daughter-in-law of Naomi	Ruth 1:4
Boaz	A man from Elimelech's clan; the kinsman-redeemer who married Mahlon's widow, Ruth	Ruth 2:1, 10
An unnamed kinsman	A man from Elimelech's clan who was nearer in relation to Naomi than was Boaz	Ruth 3:12; 4:4
Ten elders	Prominent members of the Bethlehem community	Ruth 4:2
Women of Bethlehem	Women who celebrated Obed's birth	Ruth 4:14–17
Servants, harvesters	Workers for Boaz	Ruth 2:4, 8

Agricultural Moab

Directly east of the Dead Sea was a narrow strip of cultivable land known as Moab. The area was well watered by winter rains brought by winds from the Mediterranean Sea. The porous soil held enough of the moisture for the villagers to grow cereal crops and to find good pasturage for their sheep and goats. Because of a famine in Judah, Elimelech, Naomi, and their two sons emigrated to Moab, where food was still available.

Mourning in Moab (1:3–5)

Tragedy struck in the land of Moab when Elimelech died, leaving Naomi and her sons alone. Life had to go on for Naomi, and she turned to her sons for comfort and support. The sons eventually married Moabite women, Ruth and Orpah, and the family of five enjoyed ten years together in Moab.

Tragedy struck again, however, this time with the death of both sons. Naomi was then left alone, with only her daughters-in-law, in a foreign country. The trial of famine had given way to the tragedy of death.

■ *Naomi found herself a widow in the*
■ *land of Moab. Her family had moved*
■ *there ten years before because of*
■ *famine in Bethlehem. Within a period of ten*
■ *years, Naomi lost her husband and two sons.*
■ *Only two daughters-in-law remained.*

NAOMI RETURNS HOME TO JUDAH (1:6–14)

Women in Bible times lived in a patriarchal society. Both the Old and New Testament worlds normally restricted the role of a woman primarily to the sphere of home and family. It was the father and then the husband or other male relatives who gave support and protection to women. Naomi found herself widowed in a foreign land, and without a male protector now that her husband and sons had died.

Women of the ancient world had security through their husbands and sons. In Judah, Naomi could have found support in Elimelech's extended family, known as the "father's house," but in Moab she was truly alone.

The Decision to Depart (1:6–7)

To return to Judah must have been an easy decision for Naomi to make. An older widow depended on her children to support her, but

Naomi's sons were gone, making her situation in Moab very difficult. Furthermore, there was news that God had "come to the aid of His people" (1:6) by providing food—the famine in Judah was over. It was time to go back and seek support from her deceased husband's family.

Naomi Dissuades Her Daughters-in-Law (1:8–10)

During the years in Moab, Naomi apparently enjoyed family unity with her daughters-in-law, Ruth and Orpah. They both had strong affection for Naomi and were willing to leave their homeland of Moab to journey to Judah with her.

En route to Judah, Naomi had second thoughts about taking Ruth and Orpah with her. Like her, they were widows, and as Moabite women they were more likely to find husbands and support in their own country. Since they were childless widows, they could obtain support from their "mother's home" (1:8), meaning their own father's house (Lev. 22:13).

Naomi, with as much affection for her daughters-in-law as they had for her, requested them to stay in Moab. They had dealt kindly with their deceased husbands, Naomi's sons (1:8), and now she gave them her blessing to seek rest and security with new Moabite husbands.

The two young widows were greatly saddened at the thought of parting with their beloved mother-in-law. Weeping, they resolved to join her people (1:10).

Loyal, Loving Kindness

Old Testament people understood kindness to be something more than doing a kind deed or favor for someone. The word they used for "kindness" referred to a loyal love that manifested itself not in emotions but in actions. Originally, this "loving kindness" was an integral part of covenant relations. When two persons entered into a covenant, the "loyal kindness" they showed to each other was expected as part of the covenant agreement.

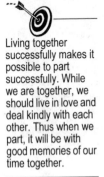
■ *Naomi's prayer was that the Lord's kindness*
■ *to Orpah and Ruth would equal their kind-*
■ *ness to her (1:8). Our view of God's goodness*
■ *is sometimes obstructed by our difficulties*
■ *and hard times. But when we look closely, we*
■ *see divine goodness beyond what we could*
■ *possibly expect.*

The Levirate Marriage Law (1:11–14)

Naomi had to explain to Orpah and Ruth what they would face if they returned to Judah with her. There, widows were protected by an Israelite custom known as levirate marriage. A brother-in-law would marry the wife of his deceased brother. Children born of this new marriage would bear the name of the deceased (Deut. 25:5–10).

The problem for Naomi was her age; she was too old to be married by a brother-in-law. Besides, even if she were to marry, it was impossible for her to have sons who could become new husbands for Ruth and Orpah. Naomi's new sons would be brothers-in-law to Ruth and Orpah, but also too young to marry. The Moabite widows' best hope for new husbands was in Moab, not in Judah.

These sobering words from Naomi drew differing reactions from the two daughters-in-law. With more weeping, Orpah returned to her own people. The other daughter-in-law, Ruth, clung to Naomi in a display of rare affection (1:14).

- *Naomi's daughers-in-law, Orphah and Ruth,*
- *wanted to join her in returning to Bethlehem.*
- *Naomi was honest with Ruth and Orphah,*
- *urging them to stay in their own country*
- *where she believed they would have a*
- *brighter future.*

THE DETERMINED LOVE OF RUTH (1:15–18)

When Ruth hesitated, Naomi reminded her that to leave Moab would mean also leaving her own gods (1:15). Ruth should return to Moab with her sister-in-law. The deity worshiped by the Moabites was named Chemosh, and Chemosh was expected to provide for Moabites as the Lord did for Judah (Judg. 11:24).

Ruth, in spite of Naomi's urging, resisted the instruction of her mother-in-law. Indeed, Ruth ended all discussion by making a solemn and firm resolution never to separate from Naomi. Naomi's people and Naomi's God would become Ruth's people and Ruth's God (1:16). Her poignant expression that she would even die in Judah showed the depth of Ruth's commitment to leave her Moabite heritage for a new land, a new people, and a new God.

Husbands and Sons

The oldest male relative was central to the Old Testament household. He was viewed as the "father," the master with ultimate authority. All who belonged to him and claimed their allegiance to him were considered part of the household—the father's house.

The authority of the "father" was significant, though he may actually have been the grandfather or great-grandfather. His responsibilities included begetting, instructing, disciplining, and nurturing. With the death of Naomi's husband and sons, her household was shattered.

In patriarchal societies the basic social unit was the clan, headed by a "father," who was the eldest male relative, perhaps a grandfather or uncle. Widows, who were without a father or husband, were social misfits, lacking a male to provide for their material needs. The most secure move for Orpah and Ruth to make was to return to their "mother's home" (1:8), where young widows could find support.

■ *Both Orpah and Ruth showed affection for*
■ *Naomi; both were willing to go with her from*
■ *Moab. Orpah, however, returned to the secu-*
■ *rity of her Moabite clan, while Ruth was*
■ *steadfast and determined to stay with*
■ *Naomi. There was nothing secure about*
■ *Ruth's decision; she herself would now*
■ *become a widow in a foreign land.*

NAOMI AND RUTH ARRIVE IN BETHLEHEM (1:19–22)

Coming home after a long absence can be a time of joyous welcome, and the people of Bethlehem were stirred over the return of Naomi. But the Naomi who had left Bethlehem more than ten years earlier, with husband and sons, was not the same Naomi who came back. Her afflicted condition caused the women who had known Naomi before to ask, "Can this be Naomi?" (1:19).

A Bitter Experience (1:20–21)

Naomi herself confirmed the people's suspicions. Jesus commanded us to love one another not just with emotion, but with a disciplined will to seek the welfare of others. That is the nature of Christian love—unselfish, loyal, and benevolent—concerned for the well-being of another. Naomi exemplified such love when she urged Ruth and Orpah to stay in Moab, caring more about their needs than her own. Ruth also loved Naomi in this way, being determined to stay by her side, although it meant leaving Ruth's homeland, the Moabite people, and the Moabite gods to worship a foreign God in a foreign land.

Naomi's feelings about her current situation were summed up by that word—*bitter*. She had left for Moab "full," with a family, but she was returning "empty," a childless widow (1:21). Her losses had left her feeling afflicted by God.

A Glimmer of Hope (1:22)

A theme that runs through the book of Ruth is the activity of God's hand in the events of life. All experiences——good and bad——come from God. So Naomi acknowledged that it was God who had afflicted her, bringing her bitterness (1:13, 21).

Yet the chapter does not end completely in gloom. Naomi returned without husband and without sons, but not totally alone. Accompanying her was a daughter-in-law who had made a sacrificial and courageous commitment to stay by Naomi's side. Perhaps Ruth would be the means through which Naomi again would experience God's grace.

Another sign of hope was the barley fields. Naomi and Ruth were returning to Bethlehem at an opportune time since the barley harvest was just beginning (1:22). Perhaps their fortunes would change, and God would restore fullness through the plentiful fields of barley.

The Meaning of a Name

In the ancient world, the meaning of a person's name held much significance. The biblical concept of naming was rooted in the ancient world's understanding that a name expressed essence. To know the name of a person was to know that person's total character and nature.

The changing of a name revealed a changing of a person's character or destiny. The personal name *Naomi* means "my pleasantness," and Naomi's life as the wife of Elimelech and mother of Mahlon and Kilion had been pleasant in many ways. But Naomi requested that her name be changed to "Mara," meaning "bitter." She was expressing the emptiness of her current situation as an aged, childless widow.

- *Our fullness in this life comes mostly from*
- *our relationships with others. When life's*
- *circumstances leave us feeling empty, we*
- *must still look to God for His blessing. Dis-*
- *appointments must not prevent us from expe-*
- *riencing the good in those around us.*

QUESTIONS TO GUIDE YOUR STUDY

1. What does it mean to conduct our relationships selflessly, placing another person's welfare and needs before our own?

2. What did Ruth say that convinced Naomi of Ruth's strong determination to go to Judah? How did Ruth show her commitment to Naomi?

3. When the circumstances of life seem to be turning against us, should we expect to find God's blessings or His punishments in our situation?

The scene changes in the second section of the book of Ruth (2:1–16). As the first chapter closed, Naomi returned to Bethlehem of Judah, accompanied by her foreign daughter-in-law, "Ruth the Moabitess" (1:22). In chapter 2, Ruth begins her challenge of faithfulness. To remain faithful to Naomi, Ruth had to support herself as a widow in a culture in which women without male support were greatly disadvantaged. She was also a foreigner who had to survive without help from her own Moabite father's house.

RUTH'S "CHANCE" MEETING (2:1–3)

Even though the Law of Moses warned the community not to take advantage of widows (Exod. 22:22; Deut. 24:17), women without husbands were among the most helpless members of society.

As soon as Naomi and Ruth returned to Judah, they faced the challenge of providing food for themselves, since they had no male to support them.

Boaz the Kinsman (2:1)

One hope Naomi had in returning from Moab was the possibility of receiving help from her deceased husband's family or clan. The story now introduces an individual by the name of Boaz, who was from Elimelech's clan. In Bethlehem, Boaz was a man of importance and wealth.

Ruth Goes to Glean (2:2–3)

Ruth took the initiative to provide food for herself and Naomi. Ruth's request that Naomi allow her to glean in the fields shows Ruth already bringing blessing to Naomi's afflicted situation. The Moabite daughter-in-law would become

Harvesttime

Among the more important crops grown in Palestine were barley, wheat, grapes, olives, and various vegetables and fruits. Crops were harvested at various times, with the barley and wheat harvests occurring from March to May. All members of the family worked at gathering the crops. It was a festive occasion, causing the prophet Isaiah to speak of joy "as people rejoice at the harvest" (Isa. 9:3). Harvest time was an opportune time for Naomi and Ruth to return to Bethlehem (Ruth 1:22).

"You shall not afflict any widow or orphan" (Exod. 22:22, NASB)

Elimelech's Clan

Boaz belonged to the clan of Elimelech. A clan was a kinship group more extensive than a family. Each clan was governed by the heads of the families that made up that clan. Several clans then combined to form a tribe. Elimelech's clan was one of the clans making up the tribe of Judah.

Laws of the Harvest

"When you reap the harvest of your land, do not reap to the very edges of your field or gather the gleanings of your harvest" (Lev. 19:9).

the Ephrathite widow's primary source of support.

Ruth looked for work, searching for a field in which she could glean behind the harvesters. By chance, she began gleaning in a field belonging to Boaz. Of all the fields Ruth could have gleaned, she picked one owned by someone from the same clan as her mother-in-law.

Was Ruth's choice of a field just by chance? The storyteller's expression "as it turned out" (2:3) intentionally exaggerates the way an onlooker might view Ruth's activity. It draws attention to the hidden reality of God's providential intervention. As Ruth went to work in the fields, God had prepared the way for her.

■ *Gleaning in Boaz's field was more than a*
■ *"lucky break" for Ruth; it was actually the*
■ *work of God veiled from Ruth's eyes. God is*
■ *often active behind the scenes of our daily*
■ *choices. Some of those "insignificant" deci-*
■ *sions we make may have very significant*
■ *results.*

BOAZ MEETS RUTH (2:4–18)

Ruth's initiative in seeking food was successful beyond expectations. She not only provided food for herself and Naomi for the present, but she also laid a foundation for their future welfare.

Boaz Inquires About Ruth (2:4–7)

As a landowner, Boaz was a wealthy relative of Naomi's. The greetings between him and his laborers, each asking the Lord's blessing on the other, picture Boaz as an important man who was well respected in Bethlehem. Words of blessing were often used as a salutation or greeting.

Ruth illustrates the axiom that "the Lord helps those who help themselves." Boaz received from his foreman a good report concerning Ruth because she was diligent. She had requested permission to glean and had worked continuously.

Perhaps Boaz was surprised at the answer to his query as to "whose young woman" Ruth was (2:5). In a patriarchal culture, the question was actually, "To what male does this woman belong?" When Ruth was identified as the Moabitess who returned with Naomi, Boaz realized that Ruth belonged to no one; she was a widow and a foreigner, although related by marriage to his own clan.

Blessings carried a stronger meaning than today's expression, "Have a good day!" In Old Testament thought patterns, the spoken word of blessing had the power of its own fulfillment. A blessing in the Lord's name released suprahuman powers which could bring to pass the content of the blessing. Ruth would discover that the Lord, not Chemosh, was the source of all blessing.

■ *Ruth's diligence and hard work attracted the*
■ *attention of Boaz. How differently her life*
■ *would have turned out, had she exerted only*
■ *a little effort, gleaning the bare minimum!*
■ *We must always put forth our best efforts,*
■ *even when the visible payoff seems small. We*
■ *do not know all that God may bring from the*
■ *seemingly insignificant tasks before us.*

Ruth Finds Favor (2:8–13)

Boaz invited Ruth to work exclusively in his fields. His generosity no doubt surprised Ruth, particularly since she was a foreigner, though he explained that he had already heard a good report about her commitment to Naomi (2:11). The Hebrews believed that God made a person favorable in the eyes of another

(Gen. 39:21), and God was directing Boaz's favor toward Ruth.

In Boaz's field, Ruth found advantages most gleaners did not have. A foreign woman could become quite uncomfortable working among male reapers, who might taunt her or subject her to an ancient form of sexual harassment. Ruth, however, could work along with Boaz's servant girls, who bundled the stalks cut by the reapers. Furthermore, Boaz warned his workers not to bother Ruth. Already she was experiencing some of the clan protection that Naomi had envisioned.

Ruth's loyalty to Naomi, demonstrated in Ruth's leaving her homeland to stay with her mother-in-law, had become known in Bethlehem and to Boaz. Loyalty is sometimes rewarded in unexpected ways, like the favor Ruth now received from Boaz. He commended her for her faithfulness and prayed that God might bless her (2:11–12).

- *Ruth found favor with a wealthy landowner*
- *because her reputation had preceded her.*
- *Boaz had heard (probably from villagers)*
- *how she treated Naomi. He heard from his*
- *foreman how hard she worked. A good repu-*
- *tation concerning our treatment of others*
- *and our diligent use of time can do much to*
- *prepare the way before us.*

Ruth's Productive Day (2:14–18)

After the talk with Boaz, Ruth presumably found her task easier, as she worked along with the servant girls. Another benefit that made her day better was Boaz's invitation to drink from the water jars that provided refreshment for the reapers.

Boaz had prayed for Ruth to be "richly rewarded" by the Lord (2:12), and he was willing to help God with the job! He rewarded Ruth with a refreshing meal: bread dipped in wine vinegar, a seasoning procured from overfermented grape wine, and roasted grain. He also ensured her work would be successful by instructing his laborers to leave stalks behind for her to glean.

In one day of gleaning, Ruth had exceeded her expectations. At the end of her work, Ruth's ephah of barley was more than enough for her and Naomi. Ruth also brought Naomi a take-home treat, having saved the leftovers from Boaz's meal.

- Naomi felt that God had afflicted her and
- made her empty (1:21). Now God was using
- Boaz and Ruth to feed Naomi. Although life's
- circumstances can leave us feeling empty at
- times, God has many ways to fill us again.

REPORTING TO NAOMI (2:19–23)

In the evening, the two widows reflected together on the day's events. Their situation looked much more hopeful. A near kinsman was providing support for the present, and might possibly for the distant future as well.

The Kinsman-Redeemer (2:19–20)

Naomi was impressed with the generosity of the landowner who had helped Ruth. Even before knowing the man's identity, Naomi called for God's blessing on him. When she learned his

Under God's Wings

The imagery of an eagle spreading its protective wings over its young is used symbolically of God (Deut. 32:11). In the same way the Lord protects His people. They find protection "under His wings" as the young eagles do under their mother's wings. The psalmists often spoke of the refuge and shelter to be found in the "shadow" of God's wings (Pss. 36:7; 57:1; 61:4). By choosing Naomi's God as her own God, Ruth indicated her desire to seek safety and security under God's wings, thus forsaking the Moabite deities (Ruth 2:12).

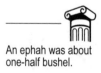

An ephah was about one-half bushel.

The Kinsman-Redeemer

In Israel's tribal structure, the kinsman-redeemer was a blood relative who assumed various "redeeming" duties. In the levirate marriage, this living kinsman became the dead relative's redeemer by raising up a male descendant in his name. He also redeemed the estate a relative might have sold because of poverty, or even a relative who had sold himself to pay a debt. Boaz is a striking example of a kinsman who fulfilled some of these redeeming duties as the kinsman-redeemer.

name was Boaz, however, she exulted in the Lord. Boaz was a close relative from her deceased husband's clan.

The credit for the day's bounty was given to God, for showing His kindness "to the living and the dead" (2:20). Naomi's mention of "the dead" probably indicates the direction her thoughts were already taking. Boaz might be the relative who would preserve Elimelech's name.

The "kinsman-redeemer" played a vital role in Israel's social support system. In the tribal structure of Israel, certain obligations were laid on this kinsman. He was expected to be a redeemer to his deceased brother by raising up a male descendant for him. To fulfill this obligation, the kinsman-redeemer must marry the dead brother's widow. Naomi knew that she herself was beyond childbearing age, but Ruth, her daughter-in-law, and also a widow, was not.

The Harvest Season (2:21–23)

The Law of Moses allowed widows to work the corners of fields during harvest, but the task could be dangerous. A woman lacking a male protector and spending long days in the fields with the crews of male reapers was virtually unprotected.

Ruth now informed Naomi that Boaz had invited Ruth to glean with his workers for the entire harvest season. The wise mother-in-law immediately urged Ruth to follow Boaz's instructions, knowing that he would provide for her safety.

The wheat harvest followed the barley harvest and continued until mid-May. The encounter of Boaz and Ruth opened the way for God to bless in an unexpected manner. For the months of harvesting, the family of two widows did not lack for food, as Ruth gleaned safely in the fields of Naomi's kinsman.

Threshing the Grain

At the end of the harvest, the sheaves of grain were brought to the threshing floor—a cleared area of stamped earth or stone. Animals, usually cattle, were driven over the spread-out stalks to trample out the grain. Often a cart wheel or a heavy sledge with small stones inserted in the bottom was drawn over the floor to hasten the threshing.

- *The good results of Ruth's gleaning caused*
- *Naomi to declare, "The LORD . . . has not*
- *stopped showing his kindness" (2:20). This*
- *outlook was far different from her earlier*
- *remark: "The Almighty has brought misfor-*
- *tune upon me" (1:21). We must always be*
- *expecting to experience God's benevolent*
- *hand in life's changing situations.*

QUESTIONS TO GUIDE YOUR STUDY

1. What is wrong with praying for God's help and then sitting tight while awaiting His divine action? How did Ruth do things differently?

2. Why did Boaz react with favor toward Ruth, even though she was a foreigner?

3. In how many different ways did Boaz's kindness exceed the demands of the law? Do you often do only what is expected, or do you go the second mile to help someone in need?

The introduction of Boaz into the story brings a glimmer of hope for Naomi and Ruth. In the third section of the book of Ruth (3:1–18), Ruth pursues that hope. With Naomi's guidance, Ruth claimed her right to a levirate marriage. But would Boaz be faithful to his deceased kinsman and fulfill the role of the kinsman-redeemer?

NAOMI INSTRUCTS RUTH (3:1–6)

As Naomi began her return trip to Judah, she was concerned for the future security of her daughters-in-law. Her prayer for them was that God would give them "rest" (1:9)—the security that a woman of that time could obtain only through marriage. Naomi's thoughts were still focused on finding rest for Ruth in the home of a new husband who would provide for her.

Naomi, as Ruth's mother-in-law, used what means she had to attempt a marriage arrangement.

The Plan to Approach Boaz (3:2–4)

Naomi's planning may seem forward and even a bit scheming to us today. Nevertheless, her actions were appropriate for that culture. A Hebrew widow could assume as her right that someone from her clan would "fulfill the duty of a brother-in-law to her" (Deut. 25:5). Apparently, the marriage custom could apply also to relatives more distant than a brother-in-law.

As Naomi saw things, the most likely candidate to be Ruth's kinsman-redeemer was Boaz. He was their kinsman; he had been remarkably kind and generous to Naomi and Ruth; and Ruth had spent two months gleaning along with his servant girls. The only question was how to make him aware of Ruth's interest as well as her own.

The opportune time arrived when the men began threshing and winnowing the grain. After an evening of winnowing, the workers feasted and then slept at the threshing floor, guarding the grain. Naomi instructed Ruth how to prepare herself properly and approach Boaz during the night at the threshing floor.

Ruth's Obedience in Faith (3:5–6)

What Ruth was asked to do in order to press Boaz on his role as a kinsman could have been embarrassing. For a woman to dress attractively, go at night to the threshing floor where the men slept, spy out the sleeping place of one particular male, and lie down at his feet had the potential of being scandalous. But Ruth had made a choice earlier that Naomi's people would be her people (1:17). Now she acted on that choice, obeying her mother-in-law's instructions.

■ *Naomi proposed a daring strategy in her*
■ *matchmaking effort. We must be bold in our*
■ *own activities. Assertive plans, when they fit*
■ *within God's will for holy living and are not*
■ *harmful to others, can become springboards*
■ *for changing our lives and the lives of others*
■ *for the better.*

RUTH AND BOAZ AT THE THRESHING FLOOR (3:7–15)

As Boaz spent the night on the threshing floor, protecting his harvest, he had a visitor, but she was not a thief: Ruth was lying at his feet.

Winnowing the Grain

Winnowing was the step in the processing of grain in which the grain was separated from the inedible chaff. The stalks of grain were thrown into the air so that the wind blew away the light scaly chaff, allowing the heavier pure grain to fall back to the ground. Winnowing left a pile of clean grain ready for grinding into flour.

Perfumes

When Ruth perfumed herself in preparation for meeting Boaz, she was following an ancient practice. The first recorded mention of perfuming is on the fifteenth-century B.C. tomb of Egypt's Queen Hatshepsut, who had sent an expedition to the land of Punt to fetch frankincense.

Perfumes were obtained from the various parts of trees. Frankincense and myrrh came from the sap or gum of the tree; spikenard from the roots; and cinnamon from the bark.

Ruth Goes to Boaz (3:7–9)

To uncover a man's feet and lie down there was both intimate and humbling. It also would be embarrassing to the man if others witnessed the scene, since Ruth was not part of his family. So Ruth approached Boaz secretly.

At some point, Naomi's plan became Ruth's plan. We do not know when Ruth herself first considered (or even dreamed of) marriage to Boaz. Was it before or after Naomi broached the subject of Boaz as a kinsman-redeemer? Regardless, in the middle of this night, Ruth was trusting God to use Boaz to answer her needs and to protect her.

Boaz was startled, for women were usually not with the men at the threshing floor during the night. In this encounter, Ruth quickly made her request, confronting Boaz with his responsibility as a kinsman. Her expression, "Spread the corner of your garment over me" (3:9), was asking Boaz for marriage and the protection it afforded.

Boaz Responds (3:10–11)

Marriage customs and relationships vary from culture to culture and from age to age, but in every intimate interaction between a man and woman there is the risk of rejection. We cannot know whether Ruth was confident or anxious or both, but she did not have to wait long for an answer.

Boaz commended Ruth for her righteous conduct (3:10). She could have pursued a younger Israelite man, even someone outside of Elimelech's clan, but she chose the older Boaz. To him, her decision demonstrated greater loyalty than her initial faithfulness to Naomi in leaving Moab. In marriage, Ruth would not

Spreading the Garment

The protection that a woman received from a man in marriage is expressed in Ruth's request of Boaz: "Spread the corner of your garment over me" (Ruth 3:9). The Lord promised the same protection to His bride, Jerusalem: "When I looked at you and saw that you were old enough for love, I spread the corner of my garment over you and covered your nakedness" (Ezek. 16:8).

think only of her own desires, but would provide an heir for her deceased husband Mahlon.

The covenant was central to understanding Old Testament family relationships. Steadfast love was the basis of the covenant which created a sense of loyalty, justice, and high regard. Ruth's personal kindness was evidence that she would uphold covenant relationships.

No cold feet delayed this marriage discussion. Boaz immediately agreed to marry Ruth according to the custom of levirate marriage. Her reputation as "a woman of noble character" (3:11) made his decision easy; although Ruth was a foreigner, she was well respected throughout the community.

The Nearer Relative (3:12–13)

Boaz's willingness to marry Ruth may seem to signal a happy ending to the story, but there was yet a new development. Something of which Ruth—and even Naomi—appeared not to have been aware was that another kinsman had the first right to redeem Ruth.

Israel's marriage custom gave priority to the nearest relative. Boaz, showing himself faithful to his community's laws, confessed the existence of "a kinsman-redeemer nearer than I" (3:12). If this unnamed kinsman declined, then Boaz promised to marry Ruth.

Boaz Protects Ruth (3:14–15)

Ruth stayed the night with Boaz at the threshing floor, but the two were awake early enough the next morning to escape notice by others. Displaying admirable selflessness, Boaz took steps to protect Ruth. He advised his servants to keep silent concerning her visit. Should the nearer

Keeping the Vow

Boaz made a vow to Ruth to marry her if the nearest relative would not. Assuring Ruth of his sincerity, Boaz declared that his vow was as certain "as the LORD lives" (3:13).

The emphasis in the Bible is on keeping a vow. An unfulfilled vow was worse than a vow never made. How certain are the vows and promises that we make to others? Can others rest assured that our verbal promises are as certain "as the LORD lives"?

kinsman decide to marry Ruth, their marriage might be tainted by gossip about her and Boaz.

As an indication of his commitment to care for Ruth as well as Naomi, Boaz supplied Ruth with a bounty of grain. Six measures of barley was such a large amount that Boaz assisted Ruth in positioning it, probably on her head, so she could carry it.

Betrothal

Ruth and Boaz began their marriage process differently than couples do today. In Bible times, the act of engagement was known as betrothal, which involved a deeper commitment than our current engagement customs. Betrothal was almost synonymous with marriage, and as binding. Israelite society recognized a moral and spiritual principle underlying the pledge of a girl to be married. The penalty under the Law of Moses for disrupting this principle, either by adultery or rape, was death by stoning (Deut. 22:23–27).

■ *The character of Ruth and Boaz was demon-*
■ *strated in their encounter at the threshing*
■ *floor. Their situation was a potential scan-*
■ *dal; yet Ruth did only as Naomi had*
■ *instructed, while Boaz acted responsibly and*
■ *unselfishly, with Ruth's best interests in*
■ *mind. When we find ourselves surrounded by*
■ *temptation, we too should behave in a man-*
■ *ner that honors God.*

RUTH REPORTS TO NAOMI (3:16–18)

The first stage of a marriage transaction was betrothal. When Naomi asked Ruth, "How did it go?" she probably hoped that marriage arrangements between Ruth and Boaz were at this stage. News of another kinsman, nearer in relation than Boaz, however, delayed the resolution of Ruth's widowhood.

The six measures of barley that Ruth brought back were another sign to Naomi that God was answering their prayers through the hand of Boaz. She was confident that because of his strong interest in Ruth, he would not let the day pass with the matter unsettled. Ruth must be patient for one more day to learn the course of her future.

N

- Boaz had promised to contact the nearer
- kinsman on the next morning and to marry
- Ruth if the other kinsmen declined. Ruth still
- was not officially betrothed, yet Naomi was
- confident that Boaz would keep his word. We
- should strive to build our own reputations
- like Boaz's, so people will trust us to do what
- we say we will do.

QUESTIONS TO GUIDE YOUR STUDY

1. How important was Ruth's reputation in Boaz's decision whether to marry her? Why is building our own reputations so important to our future welfare?

2. How did Boaz repeatedly show his desire to care for and protect Ruth?

3. Naomi always had Ruth's welfare foremost in her thoughts. How did Ruth demonstrate her respect and trust for Naomi?

The final section of the book of Ruth (Ruth 4:1–22) looks toward the future—Ruth's and Boaz's future, Naomi's future, and Israel's future as a people and nation. The characters of the story had remained faithful to each other while facing various problems—famine, widowhood, and childlessness. In the end, every problem was solved, and Ruth gave birth to a child because of faithfulness.

BOAZ APPROACHES THE NEARER RELATIVE (4:1–6)

As he had promised, Boaz took steps the next morning to determine which relative from the clan of Elimelech would become the kinsman-redeemer for the deceased Mahlon.

Meeting at the Gate (4:1–2)

For most Palestinian villages and towns, the gate was a vital place where commercial, judicial, and social activities of all sorts took place. Of current concern to Boaz was a marriage transaction, and Bethlehem's gate was the place where he would settle the matter publicly.

Soon he met the kinsman who was nearest in relation to Mahlon, Ruth's deceased husband. This relative is never described by name. When Boaz invited him to sit down for discussion, he addressed him only as "my friend" (4:1).

The interaction between Boaz and the friend was community business, and witnesses were needed for the matter to be official. During the period of the judges, the elders were prominent in the political and judicial life of Israel, so Boaz assembled ten of the town's elders to participate in their discussion.

The Town Gate

One sign that Boaz was a prosperous man with a well-ordered house was his ability to sit with the elders in the town gate. The writer of Proverbs revealed the politics of a town's gate as he commented on a noble wife: "Her husband is respected at the city gate, where he takes his seat among the elders of the land" (Prov. 31:23).

Redeeming a Relative's Property (4:3–4)

Boaz informed the friend that Naomi's fields were his to redeem. The law specified that if a poor Israelite was forced to sell some land, the nearest relative was to redeem the property by buying it back (Lev. 25:25).

We do not know in what sense Naomi was "selling" the land that had belonged to Elimelech (4:3). Was it land that Elimelech had sold earlier, but to which Naomi had legal rights to redeem if she had the money? Or was it land that still belonged to Elimelech's family, but which Naomi would be forced to sell in her current situation?

Along with informing his friend of the opportunity to redeem Elimelech's land, Boaz expressed his own desire, as "next in line" (4:4), to do so, should the friend not be interested. The friend agreed to buy the fields, possibly considering the purchase to be a bargain.

Preserving a Dead Relative's Name (4:5–6)

Boaz quickly offered additional information. If the friend bought the land, he was also obligated to marry the widow Ruth to "maintain the name of the dead with his property" (4:5). Elimelech's property would have been inherited by his sons Mahlon and Kilion, but since they had also died, legal custom called for a kinsman to marry Mahlon's widow Ruth and bear a descendant for Mahlon.

The Law of Moses did not specifically tie the redeeming of property with the custom of kinsman marriage, so the friend could decline without embarrassment. For some reason, he believed that marrying Ruth would jeopardize his own estate, so he offered the right of kinsman-redeemer to Boaz.

Naomi's Land

In ancient Israel, property was passed on to the living sons of a father, with a double portion going to the eldest son. Daughters were not to inherit from their fathers except in the absence of a son, as was the situation with Zelophehad's daughters (Num. 27:1–6). The Law of Moses did not stipulate that a widow could inherit a portion of her deceased husband's property. Yet some provisions or customs must have addressed the security of a widow, for the land that had belonged to Elimelech was now being bought "from Naomi" (Ruth 4:3, 5).

S N

- *The friend was not required technically by*
- *law to help Elimelech's family. Whatever*
- *inheritance risk he would face by marrying*
- *Ruth, Boaz would likewise face. Yet Boaz*
- *decided to go beyond the prescription of the*
- *law. To do our best for God, we must do more*
- *than what is required. Certain situations call*
- *for us to make sacrifices that others are*
- *unwilling to make.*

BOAZ THE KINSMAN-REDEEMER (4:7–12)

Before the assembled witnesses, Boaz fulfilled the custom of levirate marriage and received the blessing of the people and the elders for his role as kinsman-redeemer.

The Sandal Ceremony (4:7–8)

The understanding reached between Boaz and the friend was sealed with a ceremony—the nearer kinsman gave his sandal to Boaz. The giving of the sandal symbolized the transfer to Boaz of the friend's right to redeem.

Apparently this sandal ceremony was no longer common at the time the story of Ruth was written, so the storyteller informed his readers how it was practiced "in earlier times" (4:7).

Boaz Announces His Intentions (4:9–10)

When the friend backed out, Boaz announced that he would redeem the property and marry Ruth himself. The redemption of Naomi's family was completed: The property of Elimelech, Mahlon, and Kilion was redeemed, and Mahlon's widow was betrothed. Someday a male child born of Ruth and Boaz would preserve Mahlon's name and inherit his property.

Blessing the New Union (4:11–12)

The elders witnessed the events at the gate and offered a prayer of blessing. They asked God to give Boaz children through Ruth as abundantly as He gave Jacob through Rachel and Leah. These two women had mothered Jacob's twelve sons, who were considered the progenitors of all Israel.

The blessing also recalled Tamar, who was probably mentioned because Boaz was descended from her. Like Ruth, Tamar was a childless widow, but through her father-in-law, Judah, she bore twin sons, Perez and Zerah (Gen. 38:27–30). Now Boaz, through Ruth, would produce more descendants for Tamar.

Witnesses

Boaz called on the elders of the city to be witnesses to his act of redemption. They were to render true and faithful testimony, based on their observation, that Boaz had redeemed the land previously belonging to three deceased kinsmen—Elimelech, Mahlon, Kilion—and had agreed to marry Mahlon's widow, Ruth. As the elders declared, "We are witnesses" (Ruth 4:11), the line running from Abraham the patriarch to David the king was being drawn.

- *Boaz was faithful to the legal customs of his*
- *community and risked losing Ruth to a kins-*
- *man of nearer relation. The friend thus was*
- *given his rightful opportunity to become the*
- *kinsman-redeemer because Boaz acted righ-*
- *teously. Having "played by the rules" of his*
- *community, Boaz was much deserving of the*
- *people's blessing.*

FILLING NAOMI'S EMPTINESS (4:13–22)

Naomi's fortunes as well as Ruth's were reversed with the birth of a child—Obed. Through Boaz, the kinsman-redeemer, God filled the emptiness of Naomi with this child, ensuring the name and the future of Naomi's family.

Boaz and Ruth Give Birth (4:13–15)

God rewarded the couple by giving them the child Obed. The women of the town praised God and celebrated His gift to Naomi of a kinsman-redeemer. Through Boaz and Ruth,

More than Seven Sons

The women of Bethlehem honored Ruth with high praise in declaring her better to Naomi "than seven sons" (4:15). Sons were especially important and were considered second to the father in significance. Daughters were considered of secondary importance. Furthermore, the number *seven* symbolized completeness. A Hebrew mother could want for no greater blessing than to bear seven sons—unless it was to have a daughter-in-law as faithful as Ruth.

Naomi's life was renewed; she was no longer empty.

Ruth the Moabitess, a foreigner, became the source of much joy for her mother-in-law. Naomi had lost two sons, but Ruth had become more valuable to her than even seven sons (4:15). With the birth of Obed, Ruth was continuing the house of Naomi's son Mahlon, and now Naomi's joy outweighed her past losses.

The Ancestors of King David (4:16–22)

The women of the town recognized that the child Obed would possess Elimelech's property someday. Possibly it was in this sense that Naomi was regarded as the mother of the child. Obed would be her husband's heir, and so it could be said, "Naomi has a son" (4:17).

Naomi had gained far more than a grandson. Obed would one day become the father of Jesse, and then the grandfather of King David. Thus, he would also be an ancestor of Jesus Christ (Matt. 1:5–6).

The genealogy that closes the story shows the links from Israel's patriarchs (through Perez, the son of the patriarch Judah) to King David. One link in the genealogical chain was Obed. Because of the faithfulness of Ruth and the faithfulness of God, the promises to the patriarchs would be realized through David and his greater Son, Jesus Christ. Ruth, the foreigner, the Moabitess, would become an ancestress of Israel's Messiah.

From Abraham to Obed to David

GENEALOGY	INDIVIDUAL	TEXT
The Chronicler's Genealogy 1 Chronicles 2:1–15	Israel (= Jacob), father of Judah	2:1
	Judah, father of Perez through Tamar	2:1
	Perez, distant ancestor of Salmon	2:4
	Salmon, father of Boaz	2:11
	Boaz, father of Obed	2:12
	Obed, grandfather of David	2:12
	Jesse, father of David	2:13, 15
	David	2:15
Ruth's Genealogy Ruth 4:18–22	Perez, distant ancestor of Salmon	4:18
	Salmon	4:21
	Boaz	4:21
	Obed	4:22
	Jesse	4:22
	David	4:22
Matthew's Genealogy Matthew 1:2–6	Abraham, father of Isaac	1:2
	Isaac, father of Jacob	1:2
	Jacob, father of Judah	1:2
	Judah, father of Perez through Tamar	1:3
	Perez, distant ancestor of Salmon	1:3
	Salmon, father of Boaz through Rahab	1:5
	Boaz, great-grandfather of David through Ruth	1:5
	Obed	1:5
	Jesse	1:6
	David	1:6
Luke's Genealogy Luke 3:31–34	David	3:31
	Jesse	3:32
	Obed	3:32
	Boaz	3:32
	Salmon	3:32
	Perez	3:33
	Judah	3:33
	Jacob	3:34
	Isaac	3:34
	Abraham	3:34

Genealogy

A genealogy was a family record listing people of a particular generation. The children of each son and the children of the next generation were listed, usually for a particular purpose. Sometimes a genealogy sought to show that the final person listed had a legitimate right to hold an office or function. Such legitimation could come from the first ancestor listed. The genealogy in the book of Ruth would legitimate David as king, showing his descent from Perez, the grandson of Jacob the patriarch.

Salmon, the father of Boaz, is listed in the Gospel of Matthew as the husband of Rahab (Matt. 1:5). It is likely that Salmon's wife and Boaz's mother was "Rahab the prostitute," who was remembered by the early Christians for her faith (Heb. 11:31) and righteous deeds (James 2:25).

■ *The women of the town prayed that Boaz*
■ *would "become famous throughout Israel"*
■ *(4:14). Those prayers were answered as*
■ *Boaz became the great-grandfather of David,*
■ *the first king to unite Israel and Judah and*
■ *the first to receive the promise of a royal*
■ *Messiah in his line.*

QUESTIONS TO GUIDE YOUR STUDY

1. Ruth approached Boaz, requesting he marry her as a kinsman-redeemer. What would have happened if Boaz had kept quiet about the nearer kinsman and immediately married Ruth? Who would have been wronged?

2. Why was Boaz wise to tell the friend about Elimelech's and Mahlon's property first and about Ruth second? Could Boaz be accused of not revealing all of the facts?

3. Could Ruth have had any idea that her courtship with Boaz would result in a whole line of Judean kings? How many events in your life have made sense only years after the event itself occurred?

ESTHER

The book of Esther is named for its heroine. Esther used her prominent position as queen of Persia to save the Jewish people from destruction. Yet behind the scenes of this deliverance was divine providence. God was working by exalting Esther to be queen and by turning the tables on the Jews' enemies.

The book was intended to be read at the Feast of Purim—a festival of merrymaking, noise, and conviviality. Thus, a major theme of the book—persecution returning on the heads of those who initiate it—leads through all the details of the story to the final victory which Purim celebrates.

AUTHOR

The author of this book is unknown. Whoever wrote the story of Esther probably used sources available from the period. Information could have been drawn from the royal archives, described as "the book of the chronicles" (6:1) and as "the annals of the kings of Media and Persia" (10:2) or simply "the book of the annals" (2:23).

The author's second source of information was possibly the writings of the story's two main characters: Esther and Mordecai. Letters which Mordecai wrote to the Jews (9:20, 23) may have been preserved for a time, and decrees made by Esther and Mordecai were recorded, although it is not certain where.

Some interpreters have speculated that the author was a Persian Jew. Despite the many suggestions about who authored the book, which

Esther

The name *Esther* is probably derived from the Persian word *stara,* meaning "star." Some scholars have related the name to Ishtar, the Akkadian goddess associated with planet Venus.

includes Ezra and Mordecai, his or her identity remains hidden.

DATE OF WRITING

The date of writing is more certain, but still difficult to determine. Since the setting of the story is the reign of the Persian king Ahasuerus (1:1), who is commonly identified with Xerxes I (486–465 B.C.), the date must be placed during or after the fifth century B.C. Scholars have suggested dates of authorship ranging from the fifth century B.C. to as late as the Maccabean period (second to first centuries B.C.).

A few pieces of evidence might suggest a date some time after 300 B.C. The earliest mention of the book of Esther is found in 2 Maccabees (2 Macc. 15:36), a book which covers a period from 180 to 161 B.C. Also, Gentiles were not converted to Judaism (as indicated in Esther 8:17; 9:27) during the Persian period, but rather in the Greco-Roman period, beginning after 300 B.C.

Other evidence, however, points to a date of about 400 B.C. The author demonstrates an excellent knowledge of Persian life and customs, information that might not have been preserved centuries later. Furthermore, there is no evidence of Greek influence in the book, which suggests a date before 330 B.C. In addition, the Hebrew language observed in the book of Esther has some similarities with that of the books of Chronicles, which themselves have been dated around 400 B.C.

AUDIENCE

The book's plot includes an explanation of the origins of the Jewish Feast of Purim. Apparently, the intended audience were those Jews who participated in the celebrations of Purim.

The primary audience would have been Jews living in the diaspora, where observance of Purim was more prevalent than in Palestine. The diaspora Jews were the ones who did not return to Jerusalem as part of the "remnant." While the books of Ezra and Nehemiah tell how the exiles fared in Jerusalem, Esther tells what happened to those who stayed behind.

In Esther, those of the diaspora were shown how to be faithful to their Jewish heritage while living as honorable citizens of a gentile state. Mordecai, in particular, exemplifies loyalty to the Jewish tradition. He functioned as Esther's Jewish conscience (4:12–14), and, as a "Jew," he refused to pay homage to Haman the "Agagite" (3:1–2).

PURPOSE

A single reading of the book of Esther will not reveal the book's entire purpose. Certainly, it considers the question of destruction or survival of the Jews under persecution. And, it explains the observance of the Feast of Purim. But does the book intend to say anything about God?

In telling a story about persecution, the story addressed the problem of social and religious bigotry. Even though Haman's anti-Semitism was frightening, the Jews were warned not to escape their heritage. Indeed, their spiritual heritage preserved them as a people.

The story also told Jews why they celebrate annually on the fourteenth and fifteenth days of Adar. The Hebrew word *Purim* means "lots." While the casting of lots appeared to seal their doom (3:7), the outcome of the day selected by the lots gave them reason for celebration (9:23–26). The Feast of Purim was a Jewish commemoration of deliverance.

The Historian and Esther

Herodotus was born about 484 B.C. and became known as "the father of history." He wrote at Athens around 445 B.C., authoring the work for which he is most famous—*History of the Persian Wars*. Since Herodotus lived and wrote soon after Xerxes' reign (486–465 B.C.), he is a primary source for information on Persian history, especially for the book of Esther.

Esther is the only book in the Hebrew Bible that does not mention God's name. This does not mean, however, that the book has no theological purpose. Rather, God's subtle providence in the lives of His people is revealed. The author showed through unexpected reversals in his characters' lives how God brought about the deliverance of the Jews.

STRUCTURE AND CONTENT

The story of Esther consists of six sections, revealing a well-constructed literary piece. Ingenious writing tells the story through a flow of events, building suspense to a pivotal point. The problems and tension then cascade downward until all is resolved, yet the final solutions are unexpected. The reader is never bored.

Each section of the book before the pivotal point is matched by a corresponding section after that point. In addition, the corresponding sections are opposite each other, supporting the theme of reversal. Vashti's demotion (chap. 1) balances Mordecai's promotion (chap. 10). The decree to destroy the Jews (chaps. 2–3) is countered by the decree on their behalf (chaps. 8–9). Haman's threats against Mordecai (chaps. 4–5) are checked by Mordecai's defeat of Haman (chaps. 6–7).

These sections pivot around one event—the king's sleepless night (6:1). Before this incident, the Jews were helpless before their gentile lords. After it, the evil plan against the Jews unraveled. In the end, even the magistrates feared and honored the Jews.

LITERARY STYLE

Opinions vary as to what type of literature is represented in the book of Esther. Some scholars consider this book to be a short historical novel or short story sprinkled with historical data and names to make its message more urgent. Others think it is an attempt to write history with a free interspersion of speeches and conversation, as typical of ancient history writing. Still others insist on the historicity of every detail of the story.

Many consider the book of Esther to be a historical romance, containing elements that appear to be legend. On the other hand, they recognize that Esther has a historical nucleus. If the author did intend the book to be read as a literary fiction, it should be interpreted accordingly as one would interpret a parable or allegory without doubting its inspiration.

Other interpreters, however, believe the book's reliability as a historical witness is bolstered by its accurate and detailed knowledge of Persian life, law, and custom. Archaeological information about the architecture of the palace and about Xerxes' reign harmonizes well with the story's depictions. Furthermore, when the author invites readers to verify this story by consulting Persian annals (10:2), he indicates that it is a reliable account of the Persian Jews.

THEOLOGY

Can there be theology in a book that does not mention God and makes no reference to the Mosaic law, sacrifice, prayer, or revelation? The answer is yes, when the absence of religious language best suits the author's theological purpose. In Esther, the author expresses theology through the vehicle of story, arranging the events and dialogue to accentuate that theology.

The author of Esther omitted Israel's distinctives in order to veil God's presence. Nonetheless, the story's characters recognized divine

Esther is the only book of the Old Testament that is not found among the Dead Sea Scrolls. Apparently, the Jewish community at Qumran from 150 B.C. to A.D. 68 did not use the book, nor did they celebrate the Feast of Purim.

intervention in their lives. Although God's actions are not obvious, the author perceived that God orchestrated the salvation of the Jews. The providence of God is this author's predominant theological theme.

Another theological theme surfaces from the story's setting in the Persian court. Two different views are demonstrated on the use of wealth and power. Haman and the Jews' enemies used power for self-serving purposes, to acquire for themselves both honor and wealth. Esther and Mordecai, however, gained power because of their loyalty to the king and used it to help their people.

THE MEANING OF ESTHER FOR TODAY

Our modern experience of God is more like that of the book of Esther than the experience described in many Old Testament books. In Esther, God worked behind the scenes to bring about deliverance for His people. He did not act through spectacular plagues or a miracle at the sea as in the Exodus.

The book of Esther calls us to look at the lives of people committed to God if we want to know what God is doing to bring about deliverance in our own world. God worked through a courageous old man who refused to abandon his principles and through a courageous woman who valued the lives of her people more than she did her own life.

Today we may feel that God has abandoned us or that it is not profitable to be on the Lord's side. Through much of the book of Esther, the outlook for Mordecai and the Jews looked just as bleak. But the last chapters of the story reveal God's reversal of circumstances. We should live our lives not focused on current situations but with a view to how our story will end.

As in Esther's story, Christian citizenship demands involvement in the affairs of the state. Racial and religious bigotry can easily lead to dangerous abuses of power, but we, like Esther, must be courageous in opposing such abuses.

Our own power and influence are gifts from God. As Christians, we must use power responsibly for the benefit of God's people and creation—not for self-gratification.

The first section of the book of Esther (1:1–22) opens with the demotion of a queen. Vashti's departure created the void into which Esther would step to become the book's main character.

THE KING'S GREAT BANQUET (1:1–22)

Elaborate meals and feasts were important social events, often celebrating victories or other joyous occasions. An incident which occurred at the banquet given by King Xerxes triggered further events that would have significant consequences for Jews living in Xerxes's Persian Empire.

The Historical Setting (1:1–3)

While the book of Ruth is set "in the days when the judges ruled" (Ruth 1:1), the book of Esther is set "during the time of Xerxes" (Esther 1:1). This king, whose kingdom is described in the opening chapter of Esther, is commonly identified with Xerxes I, Persia's ruler from 486 to 465 B.C. Xerxes is the Greek name for the Persian King Khshayarsha, also known in Hebrew as Ahasuerus.

A Greek historian named Herodotus wrote about Xerxes I, providing us with information that can be compared to the book of Esther. According to Herodotus, Xerxes's father had reorganized the Persian Empire into twenty governments called "satrapies," while the book of Esther reports the size of Xerxes's kingdom as "127 provinces" (1:1). Perhaps a satrapy was subdivided into several provinces.

A mighty empire. The kingdom which Xerxes inherited from his father, Darius I, was certainly

Ahasuerus = Xerxes

The Persian king who selected Esther to be his queen is known as Ahasuerus in the Hebrew Old Testament. Ahasuerus is named again in the book of Ezra (Ezra 4:6), being listed chronologically with three other Persian kings—Cyrus (Ezra 4:3, 5), Darius I (Ezra 4:5), and Artaxerxes I (Ezra 4:7).

The chronological order of these four kings in Ezra suggests that Ahasuerus should be identified with the Persian king Xerxes I. Their reigns span a period of more than a century: Cyrus (539–530 B.C.); Darius I (522–486 B.C.); Xerxes I (486–465 B.C.); Artaxerxes I (464–423 B.C.).

Esther's Cast of Characters

CHARACTER	DESCRIPTION	SCRIPTURE
Xerxes (Ahasuerus)	King of Persia, known in Hebrew as Ahasuerus; chose Esther as his queen	Esther 1:1; 2:17
Esther (Hadassah)	A Jewish orphan girl who became queen of Persia; the cousin of Mordecai	Esther 1:2
Mordecai	A Jewish man from the tribe of Benjamin; the cousin of Esther	Esther 2:5, 7
Vashti	The queen of Persia before Esther	Esther 1:9
Haman	An Agagite man who became the highest Persian noble under Xerxes	Esther 3:1
Zeresh	The wife of Haman	Esther 5:10; 6:13
Mehuman, Biztha, Harbona, Bigtha, Abagtha, Zethar, Carcas	The eunuchs who served King Xerxes	Esther 1:10; 7:9
Carshena, Shethar, Admatha, Tarshish, Meres, Marsena, Memucan	The wise men who advised King Xerxes in matters of law and justice	Esther 1:14
Hegai	The king's eunuch in charge of the harem	Esther 2:3, 8
Shaashgaz	The king's eunuch in charge of the concubines	Esther 2:14
Bigthana, Teresh	Officers of the king	Esther 2:21; 6:2
Hathach	The king's eunuch assigned to Esther	Esther 4:5

Esther's Cast of Characters

CHARACTER	DESCRIPTION	SCRIPTURE
Parshandatha, Dalphon, Aspatha, Poratha, Adalia, Aridatha, Parmashta, Arisai, Aridai, Vaizatha	The ten sons of Haman	Esther 9:7–10

huge, described as "stretching from India to Cush" (1:1). India, the eastern boundary, refers to the Punjab, the area of Pakistan drained by the Indus River and its tributaries. Cush represented the southwestern limits of Persian power, being a nation situated south of Egypt. Xerxes was a powerful king, the ruler of one of the largest empires of Esther's time.

Wealth and power. The story begins with King Xerxes ruling in Susa (1:2). The city was captured by the Persian Cyrus the Great about 538 B.C. Later Xerxes's father made it the capital of the Persian Empire. Susa was actually the winter resort of the Persian kings; such a city added to the atmosphere of wealth that surrounded Xerxes in the Persian court.

Another aspect of the atmosphere around Xerxes was power. The king's throne was in the citadel, which was usually built at the highest and most easily defensible part of a city. Cities with such fortifications often functioned as a major military or administrative center for a region.

The king convened a royal reception in his third year, which was 483 B.C. The prominent leaders of the army from across the empire attended this banquet. Such feasts were often given to foster the loyalty of the troops.

The Magnificence of the Feast (1:4–8)

The assembly Xerxes called lasted for 180 days, half of a year, during which he displayed the splendor of his wealth. It culminated in a seven-day feast of luxurious dining and drinking. The picture of opulence in the Persian court testifies to the vast resources and power of the king. The banquet took place in the palace's garden, and it was accompanied by decor of fine linen, mosaic flooring of precious stones, and individually styled golden goblets.

Wine was typically a part of a meal in ancient times; however, due to "the king's liberality" (1:7), Xerxes's banquet was a scene of drunkenness and overindulgence. The king made sure that each of his guests could drink as much wine as he wanted (1:8).

■ *The political power of ungodly rulers may be*
■ *far-reaching, but it never reaches beyond the*
■ *reality of God. Xerxes ruled in the splendor*
■ *and strength of fortified Susa, entertaining*
■ *his subordinates with abundant wealth. Yet*
■ *behind the scene, God was active in the*
■ *events of this king's empire.*

Warring with the Greeks

Xerxes conducted military campaigns against the Greeks during his reign, continuing an effort begun by his father, Darius I. The first expedition by Darius in 490 B.C. had ended in defeat at Marathon. Avenging this loss, Xerxes launched his own campaign in 480 B.C. Although the Persians did manage to invade Greece, Xerxes's armada suffered a crippling defeat in the bay of Salamis. A land battle in 479 B.C. was also unsuccessful; Xerxes then lost interest in attempting to defeat the Greeks.

The Queen's Banquet (1:9)

Vashti, the wife of Xerxes and queen of Media and Persia, also arranged a banquet to be held in the palace. Her actions show a woman acting independently of and separately from her husband. These two separate banquets possibly represent a lack of harmony between the king and queen that would soon result in permanent separation.

King's Command

Often in the book of Esther, the Hebrew word *dāt* refers to the awesome power of the Persian king. The word appeared only in the Persian period, reflecting the customs of the Medes and Persians. The Persian king's will was law in that culture, so the king's command or royal decree was equal to the law of the land. Thus, Xerxes could declare a law allowing his guests to drink as much as they wanted.

No records have been recovered which name Vashti as the queen of any king of the Medo-Persian Empire. Herodotus identified Xerxes's queen as Amestris, not as Vashti or Esther. Though some question whether Vashti was a historical person, other possible interpretations for the queens Amestris, Vashti, and Esther exist. The name *Vashti* could have been an epithet for Amestris, since "Vashti" means "sweetheart" or "beloved." Or the Persian king may have had more than one queen.

Vashti Rejects the King's Command (1:9–12)

In a drunken stupor, the king called for Queen Vashti to "display her beauty" (1:11) before his guests. The queen refused, possibly out of decency, for it would not have been pleasant for a woman to be paraded in front of the group the king had now been entertaining for seven days. The king was not the only one who was in "high spirits from wine" (1:10).

Vashti's refusal, however, was not a simple matter of a wife not feeling "up" for a party. The king had extended an "official" invitation, sending his seven eunuchs to escort Vashti to him. Eunuchs were regarded as especially trustworthy in the ancient Near East and thus were frequently employed in royal service, especially as keepers of harems. They were the king's representatives. When Vashti refused them, she was refusing the king himself.

Furthermore, the king's reputation was at stake. His command was for Vashti to appear in her royal crown before the "people and nobles" (1:11). What a parody on Persian might: The powerful king could put on a show of wealth for 180 days and host a lavish banquet for seven days, but he could not even command his own wife. One purpose of the banquet was to impress the king's subjects, but the queen's disobedience would bring him disrepute instead.

Persian Rulers

RULER	DATES OF REIGN	SCRIPTURE
Cyrus the Great	539–530 B.C.	2 Chron. 36:22–23; Ezra 1; Isa. 44:28; 45:1; Dan. 1:21; 10:1
Cambyses	530–522 B.C.	
Darius I Hystaspes	522–486 B.C.	Ezra 4—6; Neh. 12:22; Hag. 1:1; Zech. 1:1, 7
Xerxes (Ahasuerus)	486–465 B.C.	Ezra 4:16; Esther
Artaxerxes I Longimanus	464–423 B.C.	Ezra 4:7–23; 7; 8:1; Neh. 2:1–8
Darius II Nothus	423–404 B.C.	
Artaxerxes II Mnemon	404–359 B.C.	
Artaxerxes III Ochus	359–338 B.C.	
Arses	338–335 B.C.	
Darius III Codomanus	335–331 B.C.	

The King Confers with His Wise Men (1:13–15)

Although kings had the responsibility for making the decisions, they usually consulted with their wise men. These men functioned as counselors, analyzing a situation and giving advice to the king. Yet their duties extended beyond those of an advisor; wise men were an educated class of people who also were responsible for

Seven Nobles

It is not by accident that the nobles who had "special access" to Xerxes and were "highest in the kingdom" numbered seven. The number *seven* had symbolic meaning, standing for both completeness and perfection. The practice of having seven advisers continued during the reign of Xerxes's son, Artaxerxes I. When Artaxerxes sent the priest Ezra to Jerusalem, he gave him an official letter, stating that Ezra was sent "by the king and his seven advisers" (Ezra 7:14).

preserving and transmitting the culture and learning of their society. So, within Persian society, the king's wise men were the "experts in matters of law and justice" (1:13).

The seven nobles whom Xerxes consulted represented the highest level of expertise regarding the laws of Persia. They were the "cabinet-level" advisors with "special access" to the king (1:14). They would be the ones to interpret the accepted laws of Persia concerning what should be done with a queen who disobeyed the king's command. No doubt, these seven nobles had also been among the guests of Xerxes's banquet.

The Nature of the Queen's Offense (1:16–18)

Just how serious was Vashti's refusal to appear at the king's banquet? According to Memucan, one of the seven nobles advising Xerxes, the queen's actions were quite serious. Certainly the king had been embarrassed at his banquet when his queen would not appear, but Memucan argued that the consequences of her disobedience would affect the whole community. She had not only wronged the king but also the peoples of "all the provinces" (1:16).

Memucan's reasoning reflects the male-dominated culture of his time. As he understood the situation, Vashti's act would upset the tradition of male leadership and rule in Persia. Women throughout the empire would take their cue from the queen and disrespect or disobey their husbands. To bring the matter closer to home, Memucan warned the king that the wives of the king's nobles would challenge their own husbands' authority that very day.

- Memucan was certain that Vashti had "done
- wrong" to disobey the king. Her "wrong"
- would become a greater wrong when other
- wives followed her example. When someone
- challenges our control over others, we
- quickly define such action as "wrong." Obvi-
- ously, whatever allows us to control others is
- thus "right."

Queen Vashti Is Deposed (1:19–22)

Memucan's advice to the king was to depose Vashti. She would lose her title as queen and be exiled from the king's presence. Furthermore, this punishment should be executed in the form of a royal order or decree that would be irrevocable. Vashti would not disobey again.

Decrees were proclaimed publicly by criers designated as heralds. They were also recorded in writing and stored in archives for future reference. This particular decision regarding Vashti would be "written in the laws of Persia and Media," which would make it permanent——it could not be repealed (1:19).

The not-so-hidden agenda of Memucan's counsel was to keep the women in their place. In his words, the decree would encourage wives to "respect" their husbands (1:20). Such arguments sounded reasonable to Memucan's all-male audience of king and nobles. They gladly exercised their political power for self-serving purposes. Vashti was deposed.

The king's weakness. The whole incident does not present Xerxes in a favorable light. While inebriated, he called for his queen and went into a rage when she did not come. When urged to

The Wise Men

Ancient cultures developed a distinct class of people, the sages or wise men, who were responsible for creating and preserving the wisdom of their culture. These people were part of the more educated group of their societies. They were the ones who could read and write and had the economic freedom to compile wisdom sayings.

As did Xerxes, kings consulted the wise men before making crucial decisions. Ancient persons believed that there was an orderliness to the world in which they lived and that happiness came from living according to that orderliness.

Queens and Power

The wife of a monarch could sometimes acquire a certain amount of power for herself. Female regents, who ruled alongside a male ruler, were known in the ancient Near East. Royal marriages often sealed political alliances, so daughters of more powerful allies enjoyed special privileges.

Power and influence varied from queen to queen, and the story of Esther does not picture Persian queens as having independent authority. Both Vashti and Esther were dependent on Xerxes, having little power of their own.

appease his hurt by exercising power against Vashti, the king hastily followed the lead of one of his advisors. This scene does not show a calm leader in control.

The queen's strength. Vashti showed true courage. She risked losing her high position in Persian society in order to maintain her dignity. Certainly she was aware that defying the king could result in severe consequences, yet she chose to do what was right rather than what was safe.

■ *Vashti was the first lady of one of the most*
■ *powerful empires in history. Sadly, protect-*
■ *ing our personal rights sometimes means los-*
■ *ing our positions in society. At such*
■ *moments, we must set priorities and choose*
■ *between "good" and "better."*

The King's Decree (1:22)

The decision that had been made by the king and his closest advisors was now executed throughout the empire. Advice from a wise man now became the royal decree of the king, being proclaimed to every province and to every household, in the various languages spoken in the empire.

The scene of the great banquet closes with one uncertainty: Who will be queen? Memucan's proposal was not just to demote Vashti but to replace her with someone "better than she" (1:19). Of course, by "better" Memucan did not mean appearance for Vashti was herself a woman of beauty, "lovely to look at" (1:11). The need was for a queen who would be better in obedience, yet equal in beauty.

Husbands and Wives

- *Xerxes had political power and used it to rid*
- *himself of a dissenting wife. We should not*
- *suppose from this that successful family rela-*
- *tionships can be attained by political means.*
- *Respect must be earned, not enforced.*

QUESTIONS TO GUIDE YOUR STUDY

1. Xerxes rashly agreed to depose Vashti. Why is it unadvisable to make important decisions based on feelings?

2. How can husbands and wives build mutual respect for one another? Why does offering love to a companion result in true appreciation while demanding obedience produces barriers?

3. Why should men not fear women who act independently or assertively? How can males benefit from the strengths of females?

The biblical model for marriage shared with that of Persian culture was a husband's *headship* in the home. But it did not include (at least as it was *taught*) a husband's *domination* of his wife. Competition between husbands and wives is a result of the fall (cp. Gen. 3:16). The answer provided by Christ's redemption is not autonomy of the sexes but a Spirit-empowered return to male leadership. According to John Piper, the Bible calls men to "a sense of benevolent responsibililty to lead, provide for and protect" a woman. This rules out presumed superiority and self-serving authoritarianism, and it calls for the husband to seek his wife's good spiritually, emotionally, and physically. [John Piper and Wayne Grudem, *Recovering Biblical Manhood and Womanhood* (Wheaton, Ill.: Crossway, 1991),36–45.]

The second section of the book of Esther (2:1—3:15) narrates events which culminated in another decree. The king's first decree had deposed Queen Vashti; his second, if carried out, would destroy the Jewish people in the Persian Empire.

Two episodes introduce new characters into the story. The exaltation of Esther provided for Xerxes a new queen, who happened to be Jewish (Esther 2). The evil plot by Haman raised a threat to the survival of the Jews (Esther 3). A third new character, Mordecai, linked the two episodes through his role as Esther's cousin and Haman's hated enemy.

ESTHER'S RISE TO QUEEN (2:1–18)

Esther's story is a "rags-to-riches" tale of a Jewish orphan raised by her uncle in Persia who became queen of the Persian Empire. Her dramatic rise was possible partly because of Queen Vashti's refusal to appear at her husband's banquet. The courageous Vashti would be followed by an even more courageous Esther.

The Search for a Queen Begins (2:1–4)

Some time after the banquet, Xerxes "remembered Vashti." Again, the king is not presented favorably. His anger had passed and now he reflected on Vashti. Perhaps he missed her and regretted his decree to depose her, but his rash decision, made in anger, could not be undone.

At his attendants' advice, Xerxes ordered a search for Vashti's successor. The plan called for gathering "beautiful young virgins" from throughout the empire and bringing them into the king's harem at Susa. The process was not exactly what we would call "courtship"; the women selected would be taken from their homes and confined to the harem.

The eunuch in charge of King Xerxes' harem was named Hegai, a Persian name of unknown meaning. All of the young women selected as prospective queens were placed under Hegai's care.

The "beauty treatments" which the women received might seem like a benefit (2:3). Rather, they were another sign of Xerxes's use of power for self-gratification. The king snatched the most beautiful girls from their families and then treated them not as persons but as "things," which he beautified for his own enjoyment. The whole affair was to find one woman "who pleases the king" (2:4).

Esther Enters the Palace (2:5–9)

Esther was among those brought to the king's palace because of her exceptional beauty——she was "lovely in form and features" (2:7). We learn of Esther, however, through a relative, Mordecai, who was Esther's foster parent and elder cousin. A short history of Mordecai reveals something about Esther that figures prominently throughout the rest of the story: her Jewish nationality.

Through Mordecai the Jew, we are introduced to his cousin Hadassah, the name by which Esther is known in Hebrew. We are not told how Esther's parents died, but God's providence is indirectly revealed in Mordecai's care for his orphaned cousin, whom he adopted as "his own daughter" (2:7).

Esther and Hegai. The book of Esther does not speak directly of God's participation in the lives

The Eunuch

The Greek word which is translated "eunuch" means literally "one in charge of a bed." The expression refers to the beds of a king's concubines, for eunuchs were appointed by kings to be in charge of the royal harem.

Hadassah

Esther's Hebrew name was "Hadassah." This was possibly her original name, in which case it would have come from the Hebrew word for "myrtle." Some scholars suggest that "Hadassah" was a title given to Esther. The Akkadian language has a similar title meaning "bride," which is applied to the goddess Ishtar.

Esther Meets with the King

THE MEETING	THE RESULT	SCRIPTURE
Esther auditions before King Xerxes	Esther attracts the king and wins his favor. Esther is chosen to be queen.	Esther 2:15–18
Esther approaches King Xerxes without being summoned	The king receives Esther and offers to fulfill any request. Esther asks the king to attend her banquet and to bring Haman.	Esther 5:1–5
Esther's first banquet	The king offers to fulfill any request for Esther. She asks the king and Haman to attend her banquet on the next day.	Esther 5:6–8
Esther's second banquet	The king offers to fulfill any request for Esther. She beseeches the king to save her and her people.	Esther 7:1–5
Esther asks the king to overrule Haman's decree	The king grants Esther and Mordecai authority to write a decree in his name on behalf of the Jews.	Esther 8:3–8

of His people. Yet God's presence is hinted at often. Esther was only one of many girls who were brought to the palace, but she was the only one befriended by Hegai, the eunuch charged with caring for the selected virgins. Because of God working through Hegai, Esther was situated in the "best place in the harem," as well as assigned seven maids to attend to her needs (2:9).

Kish

Mordecai is listed as a descendant of the Benjaminite named Kish. Some scholars think that this Kish was the father of King Saul (1 Sam. 9:1–2). If Kish was the one "taken captive with Jehoiachin" (Esther 2:6) in 597 B.C., then he was not the same Kish who fathered Saul around 1100 B.C. Mordecai, like Saul, was from the tribe of Benjamin and could have had a father named after Saul's father.

Humans are often the instruments through which God expresses His intervention in human affairs. The commissioners appointed by the king searched "every province of his realm" and chose Esther to be one of many candidates. Of the many, it was Esther who won favor with Hegai. God was at work in the selection process.

Mordecai's Concern for Esther (2:10–11)

Since many girls had been selected, each girl faced very slim odds of becoming queen. Mordecai wisely coached Esther to keep her Jewish identity a secret. The Jews had been displaced from their homeland to become a minority people in Persia. There was no chance for a Jewish man to become Persia's king, and almost as little for a Jewish woman to become queen.

The story does not specify exactly why Mordecai told Esther to hide her Jewish background. Possibly he was excited about the advantages the Jews might enjoy if Esther were chosen by Xerxes to share the royal throne. It would be unfortunate if the king rejected Esther simply because she was Jewish.

Another possibility, though, is that Mordecai simply feared for Esther's safety. She was now under the care (and authority) of the royal harem. Any anti-Semitic feelings that arose in the empire would spell trouble for a Jewish girl in the palace. Mordecai's anxiety over Esther is evident, since he visited the harem courtyard each day to check on her welfare (2:11).

Had Esther revealed her nationality, the chances of her being chosen queen would have been greatly diminished, if not eliminated. Herodotus wrote that the Persian king was supposed to search for a new queen from among the foremost Persian families.

Concubines

Filling the role of secondary wives, concubines were generally taken by tribal chiefs, kings, and other wealthy men. Being a king's concubine meant belonging to him as his property.

- Mordecai was the mastermind behind
- Esther's rise to power. When we face crucial
- turning points in life, the advice of those who
- are older and wiser and who truly care for
- our welfare is invaluable.

The Candidate's Procedure (2:12–14)

The process by which the girls would meet the king was extensive. A full year of beauty treatments enhanced their appearance. Cremes, ointments, and perfumes were especially important in hot climates. Creams protected the skin against the heat of the sun and counteracted body odors. Ointments were a part of hygienic cleansing.

Apparently, each girl had only one chance to win the king's attention. After an evening visit with the king, a girl was returned to a different part of the harem and remained there, possibly forever. Only if the king requested her specifically would she visit him again.

Only one girl would become queen; the rest were destined to become concubines of the king. A concubine was something of a secondary wife. She was the king's property. If he should not call for her again, her life became that of a perpetual widow. Her relationships with males were primarily any interaction she had with Shaashgaz, the eunuch in charge of the king's concubines.

N

■ *Being chosen as a candidate for queen was*
■ *not necessarily a good thing. The girls lost*
■ *their freedom to come and go at will. They*
■ *were separated from all previous relation-*
■ *ships. The odds were overwhelming that they*
■ *would never marry. True injustice occurs*
■ *when one human abuses the lives of others to*
■ *satisfy personal pleasures and desires.*

Esther Prepares to Meet the King (2:15–16)

The one year of purification required for an audience with the king, as well as the many virgins involved, made for a lengthy selection process. By the time Esther was ready to be received by King Xerxes, in the seventh year of his reign (2:16), four years had elapsed since Queen Vashti's dethronement.

Just how long Esther prepared for her meeting with Xerxes is unknown. The banquet was held in 483 B.C.; Esther went before Xerxes in 479 B.C. But the timing of events in between is uncertain. We do not know how many months passed before Xerxes "remembered Vashti" (2:1) and began the search for a new queen.

Even during the time of preparation, God was present in almost imperceptible ways. The virgins had little independence; however, each girl was allowed to choose something from the harem (probably adornment) to take on her visit with Xerxes. Esther chose only what Hegai suggested she take. Hegai, as the king's eunuch, likely possessed insight into what would please the king.

One crisis that no doubt caused a major interruption was the war Xerxes fought against Greece in 480–479 B.C.

The western expedition against the Greeks by Xerxes's Persian ships ended in disaster at Salamis in 480 B.C. The king's selection of Esther as queen occurred about one year after this debacle.

■ *God worked behind the scenes in small ways.*
■ *Esther helped herself by following Hegai's*
■ *advice, but God guided Esther to listen and*
■ *learn. Hegai's advice provided Esther with*
■ *an advantage, but God had first given Esther*
■ *favor with Hegai.*

Esther Succeeds Vashti as Queen (2:17–18)

Esther won the king's approval and became Persia's new queen. The Jewish orphan rose to the position of first lady of a foreign empire; this significant event would influence everything that occurs in the rest of the story.

A theme that repeats itself during Esther's rise is her finding "favor" with others. Right from the start, she won the favor of Hegai the eunuch (2:9). As she prepared for her encounter with the king, she won the favor of all who saw her (2:15). When at last she appeared before Xerxes, she won his favor "more than any of the other virgins" (2:17). Esther was beautiful, but it was not her physical attractiveness alone that "won favor." What others saw was God's presence which gave her an attraction beyond her natural self.

Another recurring theme is the contrast between festival and fasting. The book began with Xerxes's elaborate seven-day banquet. The selection of Esther to be queen was another occasion for feasting. This banquet would be "Esther's banquet" (2:18). Characteristic of the festival was celebration: This was a time for a holiday and abundant gifts.

Mordecai Foils a Conspiracy (2:19–23)

Mordecai may have been in the king's service as a gatekeeper (2:19). For some reason, he was at the king's gate when he overheard a plot against the king's life. Xerxes's military losses at Salamis in 480 B.C. had caused disaffection within his empire, and unrest possibly led some to plan his death.

Through Esther, Mordecai reported the plot, and the two culprits were executed. The incident would have significance far beyond an uncovered conspiracy. Mordecai's heroism was recorded (2:23), and Mordecai himself began to realize the new power Esther had in the royal court. Both Mordecai and Esther showed by this incident that they were loyal to King Xerxes.

The New Queen

Esther overcame great obstacles to become Persia's queen. She was a foreigner and a poor female in an empire dominated by Persian males. With God, however, our opportunities are not limited by our gender, our nationality, or our lack of wealth. When we commit to do God's will, God works through us in ways that confound the world's expectations.

QUESTIONS TO GUIDE YOUR STUDY

1. Why was it "right" for Esther not to reveal her Jewish background?

2. Esther humbly obeyed her cousin Mordecai, not only while she was in the harem, but even after becoming queen. What does this reveal about Esther's character and attitude?

3. How was God working in the lives of Esther and Mordecai to put them in a position to serve others?

ESTHER 3

The search for someone to replace Queen Vashti introduces the story's main protagonist: the Jewish Esther who was chosen for the prominent position of queen of Persia. Her rise to power is immediately followed by the rise of another. Haman is introduced as the story's main antagonist, as he became the grand vizier under King Xerxes.

HAMAN'S MURDEROUS PLAN (3:1–15)

The theme of power is continued in the person of Haman the Agagite, who became second in position to the king. Haman was not only powerful, but also a fierce enemy of the Jews. A power struggle began: Esther used her influence as queen on behalf of the Jews, while Haman devised a plot to exterminate them.

The King Promotes Haman (3:1–2)

Haman was one of the king's nobles, so he had possibly been at the king's banquet which Vashti refused to attend. We do not know why the king chose to appoint Haman over all the other nobles, but the appointment suggests that he was an individual with strong leadership abilities.

Important for understanding the tension between Haman and Mordecai is the description of Haman as "the Agagite." Apparently, the term *Agagite* meant a descendant of Agag. King Agag was ruler of the Amalekites, a tribal people living in the Negev and in the Sinai peninsula when Israel first came to the Promised Land. So "Agagite" is probably a synonym for "Amalekite."

Hammedatha

All that is known of the person named Hammedatha is that he was the father of Haman. His name seems to be a genuine Persian name, appearing also in tablets discovered in the Persian city of Persepolis. *Hammedatha* means "given by the gods."

Anyone familiar with the history of the Jewish people would understand why Mordecai the Jew might refuse to bow to an Agagite/Amalekite. Israelites and Amalekites fought each other continuously, before Israel had entered Canaan and after they had settled there. The conflict between these two peoples was an ancient feud which resurfaced when Mordecai refused to honor an Agagite (3:2).

Agag

"Agag" was a common name among Amalekite kings much as "Pharaoh" was among Egyptian rulers. A most bitter incident between Israel and Agag involved the prophet Samuel and King Saul. Saul had destroyed all the Amalekites except King Agag (1 Sam. 15:8–9). Since the Lord had ordered the complete destruction of the Amalekites, Samuel rebuked Saul for his disobedience, and then executed Agag (1 Sam. 15:33).

The scene at the king's gate when Haman arrived was filled with official protocol. At Persepolis, one of Persia's four capital cities, archaeologists found a large, spacious entrance to the king's palace, and Susa's palace probably was constructed similarly. Although many people could gather in the immense area called "the king's gate," the arrival of Haman would not go unnoticed. The grand vizier was similar to a prime minister, and the king had ordered all other royal officials to bow in respect for the office.

Haman Burns with Anger Against Mordecai (3:3–6)

Exactly why Mordecai refused to bow to Haman is not told in the story. Officials observing Mordecai's behavior wondered why he would ignore the protocol ordered by the king. Certainly, the reason could have been political. Mordecai was a Jew from the tribe of Benjamin (2:5), and the Jewish Targums said that a Benjaminite should never show reverence to someone descended from the Amalekites.

Yet Mordecai might have had religious reasons also. For the Persians, bowing to the grand vizier was considered slightly more than an act of reverence; it became an act of worship when they imagined the vizier himself to be divine.

As Daniel had declined to worship the Persian king Darius (Dan. 6), so Mordecai's Jewish faith may have prevented him from bowing to Haman.

Possessing power is not necessarily evil, but abusing power by exercising it to the harm of other persons is a trampling of justice. With his authority as grand vizier, Haman could have dealt with Mordecai through various channels. (A novel solution would have been to meet with Mordecai in an effort to understand his perspective as a minority.) Haman's immediate response of rage reveals his arrogance and pride.

Mordecai simply would not bow to Haman. We can write lengthy creeds and declare our beliefs in eloquent statements of faith, but the true test of our belief in God comes through real-life temptations. What do we do when circumstances pressure us to substitute an earthly authority figure for God?

Even more revealing is Haman's masterminding of a plot to exterminate all the Jews. Only an extreme lust for power and position, coupled with hatred of certain people, would cause someone to consider taking so many lives. The plot for the rest of the story now unfolds: The king's most powerful official would have the Jews destroyed; the king's queen is herself a Jew. A high-level power struggle is about to begin.

In our various societies and communities, it is never wrong to honor individuals who perform noteworthy deeds or contribute significantly to their fellow citizens. But we must remember that God deserves honor and worship from us that is higher than any respect or praise we might pay to human leaders.

Haman Lays Out His Plan (3:7–11)

We do not know how long it took Haman to formulate his evil plan. The story now moved forward to Xerxes's twelfth year, which was 474 B.C. Esther had been queen for five years.

The month of Nisan was the first month of the new year, and the custom in Persia called for the casting of lots at that time. Lots were cast to determine which month during the year would be most favorable for significant events.

Casting lots was a practice in the ancient Near East to determine the will of the gods. We do not know the shape or material of these objects, but priests and magicians made difficult and significant decisions by casting lots on the ground or drawing them from a receptacle. Whatever answer the lot gave was considered an omen from the deity. Haman was willing to wait almost a whole year to execute his plan, since the lot selected the twelfth month—Adar.

The interchange between Xerxes and Haman reveals the weakness of this king and the shrewdness of his grand vizier. Mighty Xerxes, draped in royal splendor, was a weak, easily manipulated monarch who was illinformed about the events of his own kingdom. Haman wove together truth, exaggeration, half-truth, and lies in his effort to win the king's approval of his plan.

The truth. Haman described the Jews as "dispersed and scattered" throughout the kingdom (3:8). Although Haman might have exaggerated, the story repeatedly emphasizes how widespread the Jews were in the empire (8:11, 13; 9:16).

The half-truth. Characterizing the Jews as separate and having different customs was only partially true. Certainly the Jews, with their emphasis on the Law of Moses, were distinct among the peoples of the Persian Empire. But Haman twisted the truth by painting the Jews as different "from … all other people" (3:8).

"Lot"

The Hebrew word *pur* comes from the Babylonian word *puru,* both words meaning "lot."

Sacred Lots

While the Persians cast the *pur,* Israel had its own form of sacred lots. The Urim and Thummim were objects Israel, and especially the high priest, used to determine God's will or to receive a divine answer to a question.

An illustration of the Urim and Thummim in action was Saul's use of them to determine who had broken his vow during battle (1 Sam. 14:41–45). They were perhaps drawn or shaken from a bag. One object gave one answer. The other lot gave another answer. Whichever lot came out first was probably understood to be God's answer.

When we plan to persecute certain people, we often begin by stereotyping them as "different" from all others, and thus deserving of persecution.

The lies. Accusing all of the Jewish people of disobeying the king's laws was untrue. Mordecai's failure to follow protocol hardly qualified as defiant disobedience of the king. And to transfer guilt upon a whole group of people based on the actions of one member of the group was outright fraud and deception.

The bribe. Haman obviously was wealthy, offering about 375 tons of silver to cover the expense of his plan. Wealth and corruption are powerful partners. Wealthy evildoers do not hesitate to use their resources in any manner that will accomplish their evil objectives.

Haman's proposal was apparently persuasive, and the king agreed to permit the mass murder by official decree. By giving the signet ring to Haman, the king was granting him the highest authority in the land (3:10). The royal signet ring empowered subordinates to act for the king, so Haman possessed the power to do whatever he pleased. Never during Haman's presentation were the Jews mentioned by name; Xerxes had delegated power to his grand vizier without knowing the full consequences of his decision.

By saying to Haman, "Do with the people as you please," Xerxes showed he did not fully respect the dignity of human life. He could so easily allow a group of people to be destroyed on the accusation of one man. Had he valued human beings, he would have investigated the nature of the people's disobedience before agreeing to their mass destruction.

The Edict Is Issued (3:12–15)

Haman lost no time in putting his plan into effect. On the thirteenth day of the month, he had the royal secretaries write out the orders that would be given to the leading officials of the empire: the satraps, governors, and nobles. Since the king's signet ring was used to seal these orders, they would carry the same authority as if the king had written them himself.

Couriers raced throughout the empire to deliver the decree that called for the Jews to be destroyed eleven months later, in the month of Adar. Furthermore, the Jews' possessions would be plundered. Although Haman had offered to finance his proposed scheme, he probably anticipated the wealth that might be confiscated from the Jews after their demise.

The specific day of destruction, the thirteenth day of Adar, was significant for the Jews, since it fell one day before an important Jewish festival. On the fourteenth day of Adar, Jews began the celebration of Passover, the feast that commemorated their deliverance from Egypt. Had God delivered their ancestors from Egypt only to let these descendants perish in Persia?

A strange contrast ends the tragic events of chapter 3. In the royal palace, the evil perpetrator confidently celebrated with the king over a meal (3:15). But outside the calm dinner atmosphere of the palace, the common people in all the provinces were shocked by this cold-blooded decree.

Mail Couriers

Persia's postal system cannot compare to ours today, but it was one of the most efficient systems of ancient times. Good communications called for good roads, and Persia's development of roadways encouraged contacts between peoples within the empire. Ideas and goods could move hundreds of miles with little restriction.

■ *Putting loyalty to God and to godly tradi-*
■ *tions above loyalty to human rulers may*
■ *cause personal and even national persecu-*
■ *tion. At those times we should remember that*
■ *we express our belief in God by our actions*
■ *and our public witness more effectively than*
■ *we do with our verbal declarations of faith.*

QUESTIONS TO GUIDE YOUR STUDY

1. Mordecai identified himself as a Jew, thereby facing a threat from Haman. How many situations can you list in which being identified with God's people brings persecution or hardship?

2. Why did Haman hate the Jewish people? What beliefs and customs of the Jews were different than Haman's?

3. After consenting to Haman's plan, the king sat down to drink, but what did he fail to realize concerning his own family?

In the third section of the book of Esther (4:1—5:14), Haman's evil plotting against Mordecai reaches its climax. What began with anger over Mordecai's actions (3:5) evolved into a plan to eliminate Mordecai by eliminating his people (3:6). Haman's arrogance and rage, however, were greater than his patience, and he decided to kill Mordecai immediately rather than waiting until the month of Adar.

ESTHER ACCEPTS HER DESTINY (4:1–17)

Esther's position as queen could possibly enable her to save the Jews. The task would not be easy, though. Haman, her opponent, was the second most powerful man in the empire. Furthermore, because of Persian customs and laws, she could jeopardize her own position as queen if she made a wrong move. There were tough choices ahead.

Mordecai's Bewilderment (4:1–3)

The fate of the Jewish people was now sealed with the king's signet ring. Evidence of the reality of this threat could be seen in the royal couriers who were scurrying throughout the empire, proclaiming the edict's provisions and its timing—the month of Adar. Eleven months can seem like a short time to people who are facing their own execution. The story reaches its lowest point as the edict is publicized.

For all of the Jewish people, this was a time of bewilderment. Over a century had passed since they had been exiled from their homeland. Those who had not returned to Judah in

538 B.C. had settled into a new life in a foreign land. Now they were to lose life itself.

When Mordecai learned of the plot, he joined all the Jews in mourning, fasting, and wearing sackcloth and ashes. This spontaneous act of grief evidenced the solidarity of the people. It also showed their faith in their God, for the custom of sackcloth and ashes included prayers of confession and worship.

Public expressions of mourning were common in the Persian Empire. Herodotus recorded how Xerxes's defeat at the battle of Salamis caused the Persian people to tear their clothes in a display of grief. Nevertheless, Persian law forbade the wearing of sackcloth inside the king's gate (4:2). Today's politicians frequently claim to "feel the pain" of the people, but when pain is not permitted within the privileged precincts, the people rightfully question whether any "feeling" is there.

Displaying Grief

In ancient times, various practices and emotions were associated with the death of a loved one or of other catastrophes and tragedies. Weeping was then, as now, the primary indication of grief. Using imagery of weeping, the psalmist expressed the depths of grief: "My tears have been my food day and night" (Ps. 42:3).

Wearing Sackcloth

Besides weeping, people in mourning often disordered their appearance, probably to convince onlookers that the mourner was really grieving. Sometimes they tore their garments. The women often wore black or somber material. Frequently, mourners wore sackcloth, a garment of coarse material fashioned from goat or camel hair.

- *God's actions and presence are not obvious in*
- *the book of Esther, but they are assumed.*
- *Prayer commonly occurred with fasting,*
- *which was practiced to seek a deeper experi-*
- *ence with God. Crises and moments of great*
- *distress test our desire to know God and*
- *experience His presence.*

Esther Cares for Mordecai (4:4–11)

Through the mourning of Mordecai, we learn some details of Esther's life as queen. During her five years in the palace, she had kept her Jewish nationality secret. Hiding her identity meant sacrificing close personal contact with her cousin Mordecai, yet she was able to communicate with him through her trusted staff.

Maids and eunuchs assigned to Esther were the people with whom she most frequently interacted. Some of these assistants apparently were highly trusted to preserve Esther's secrecy. Through them, Esther could keep in touch with Mordecai without her Jewish background becoming known in the palace.

Esther inquires of Mordecai (4:4–5). The queen had not yet learned of the royal decree against her people. When she heard that Mordecai was wearing sackcloth, she sent him clothing to take care of his needs. Esther was about to discover that Mordecai's "needs" were greater than clothing.

When Mordecai refused the gift of clothes, Esther sent her eunuch Hathach to find out exactly what was affecting her cousin. Hathach certainly was a trusted servant. In his role as messenger between Esther and Mordecai, Hathach probably became aware of the queen's Jewish nationality.

Mordecai pleads with Esther (4:6–8). Hathach and Mordecai were able to speak with each other in the large square outside the king's gate; there they would not attract the attention of Haman's associates. The information that Mordecai returned with Esther's messenger included a copy of the edict and the "exact amount of money" Haman had offered the royal treasury. This news would impress upon Esther the urgency of the situation.

Hathach brought more than information to Esther; he also relayed Mordecai's plea for help. The plea introduces the reason Esther was selected as queen: Mordecai recognized that

Hathach

Esther assigned one of her servants to find out why Mordecai was troubled. The servant, a eunuch, was named appropriately for his task, which involved several trips back and forth between Esther and Mordecai. The name *Hathach* is perhaps of Persian origin and means "runner" or "courier."

Esther's position and power as queen was a gift to be used for her people's deliverance (see 4:14). It was time to end the secrecy about her Jewish background.

Esther explains her predicament (4:9–11). Sending Hathach back to Mordecai, Esther explained that she could not approach the king on her own initiative. Persian law prescribed death to anyone entering the inner court without the king's invitation. Furthermore, the king had not called for Esther for thirty days; it was Xerxes's choice, not Esther's, when they would meet again.

Mordecai Challenges Esther (4:12–14)

Presumably, it was Hathach who returned to Mordecai with Esther's concerns. Mordecai responded to Esther with a warning: As a Jewish woman, her own life was in jeopardy. She could not expect to escape the tragedy facing the Jews by hiding in the royal palace. Certainly she would risk her position and life by entering the king's inner court uninvited. But if she did nothing, she, too, would perish as a Jew.

Without mentioning God's name, the book of Esther again alludes to His providential care of His people. Mordecai was convinced that God could save His people by another means if Esther did not act. Yet he challenged her with an idea also based on God's providence: Perhaps her exaltation in the palace had a holy purpose. Perhaps she had been chosen queen in order to complete a unique task at "such a time as this" (4:14).

Herodotus writes in his *History* that Persian kings did have a law, as Esther describes, against approaching the king without being summoned. According to Herodotus, another provision of the law permitted someone desiring an audience with the king to request one through a messenger. Possibly Esther was unaware of this provision.

- Positions of influence bring responsibility to
- act for God's people. Our opportunities to
- serve may not affect the lives of an entire
- nation, as Esther's did. Nevertheless, each
- opportunity to serve will affect someone in
- some place. Like Esther, we, too, must accept
- our tasks.

Esther Makes Her Choice (4:15–17)

If Hathach was the person relaying all these messages between Esther and Mordecai, he must have realized the gravity of their discussions. Queen Esther was at a turning point. Why had she become queen? If she violated Persian law and custom to approach the king, would she be banished? Vashti was gone; would Esther be next?

The remainder of the story of Esther could be told in either of two very different ways, for the ending hinges on Esther's decision. The courage of Vashti to refuse to display herself and the courage of Mordecai to refuse to worship an arrogant leader is now matched by Esther's courage to save her people.

God's providence is understood in Esther's call for fasting. She requested a communal fast by all the Jews to petition God, and she even had her maids fast with her. Such intense fasting also presumed intense prayer, so Esther realized the need for God to intervene on her behalf.

The story takes a dramatic turn with Esther's decision to go to the king. Her words "I will go" (4:16) reveal her courage to serve. Her resolution, "If I perish, I perish," shows her confidence in God's will.

Fast for Me

Esther faced an uncertain and potentially difficult situation: How would the king react when she entered his presence? In times of trial, we must not attempt to deal with circumstances on our own. We need God's intervention and the spiritual support of our fellow believers. The next time you are struggling, follow Esther's example by asking others: "Fast for me" (Esther 4:16).

$\mathcal{S}$Ν

- *Times of danger force us into action and*
- *raise the question: What action is best? God's*
- *people must not act first and pray later, nor*
- *simply just act. They must pray for divine*
- *guidance, seeking to know the course of*
- *action that will honor God.*

QUESTIONS TO GUIDE YOUR STUDY

1. Can you see God's purposes in some of the perplexing circumstances of your life? How do you know that God is involved in life's events?

2. Does God ever force an individual to serve His purposes? Why would God rather find someone else to carry out His will?

3. What priorities did Esther have to set in order to make her decision? What preparations did she make once the decision was made?

Following her vow of devotion, Esther took the lead, devising her own scheme to outmaneuver Haman. Ironically, Haman unwittingly devised a scheme of his own that would hasten his own end.

ESTHER'S BANQUET AND HAMAN'S FOLLY (5:1–14)

In two separate episodes, Esther and Haman pursued opposing goals. Esther's loyalty to the king and favor with him became her source of power. Abusive power became Haman's noose with which he eventually hanged himself.

Esther Enters the King's Presence (5:1–4)

The stakes were high as Esther moved toward the palace's inner court. She was breaking Persian law to approach the king unsummoned, and the penalty could mean her death. At the very least, she would be deposed, as her predecessor had been. Still, Esther walked with determination until she stood in the king's view.

No one could have been better prepared for this moment. Fasting and praying for three days had strengthened her spiritually. She had also made use of her natural resources. King Xerxes was more attracted to Esther than any other woman (2:17), and Esther had enhanced her beauty, dressing in the royal robes.

Esther's one hope was the king's gold scepter. As part of the royal regalia, the scepter was extended to a visitor to signal the king's approval of the visit and to allow the person to approach the throne. The prayers of God's people were answered because Xerxes, raising his scepter, received Esther without incident.

The Royal Scepter

The official staff or baton of a king, his scepter, was symbolic of his authority. Scepters were decorated elaborately with gold and precious stones. The type of scepter usually differed from one kingdom to the next. Shapes varied from wide, short maces to long, slender poles.

The king knew immediately that Esther had an important reason for coming to him in such a bold manner. His offer to grant her any request, even "half the kingdom," was, of course, a figure of speech. Yet it showed the king's commitment to Esther. The queen herself, showing her confidence in God's providential hand, had already prepared a banquet. At this point, her only request of the king was for him to come to the feast—and to bring Haman.

■ *Self-giving action is rewarded in unex-*
■ *pected ways. When Esther approached the*
■ *king, risking her own security and safety,*
■ *she was rewarded by the king's favorable*
■ *response. We must be willing to act for God,*
■ *not being concerned about what rewards*
■ *might result, but being confident of God's*
■ *help and presence.*

The First Banquet (5:5–8)

The king did not hesitate to bring Haman to Esther's banquet, fulfilling her request. The queen's uninvited entrance to the king's inner court had made Xerxes curious about what was on her mind. Her additional request that the kingdom's second most powerful official also attend the banquet must have increased the king's curiosity.

Once Esther's guests had enjoyed their fill, Xerxes again implored the queen to make her petition known. Again he emphasized his desire to satisfy Esther's needs, figuratively offering her "up to half the kingdom" (5:6). Esther wisely delayed her request until the next day, a maneuver most likely intended to heighten the king's interest in her eventual petition. The delay for more feasting did indeed increase the suspense.

Pride Goes Before a Fall (5:9–14)

Haman left the banquet in a happy mood, having just enjoyed a private meal with the king and queen. His joy, however, was tempered by his fury for "that Jew Mordecai" (5:13). Mordecai had probably removed his sackcloth; thus, he could return to the king's gate. On this occasion, Haman managed to control himself, although Mordecai easily got under Haman's skin.

This incident shows the fragility of Haman's emotions. One sighting of Mordecai and Haman lost his glow. Haman's pride required continuous stroking, something Mordecai refused to provide.

Haman's real values became evident in his boasting to family and friends. Wealth, many sons, honor, and position were the things that were most important to him. Boasting of "many sons" (5:11) does not necessarily indicate that Haman was a caring family man. In the ancient Near East, children were considered the property of the father, and sons were valued more highly than daughters. So having many sons helped build Haman's already-over-inflated ego, as did having wealth, honor, and position.

Sadly, some people are never satisfied and never have "enough." In addition to his many earthly benefits, Haman boasted of his invitation to eat with the king and queen. Still, Haman's need for honor and praise could not tolerate Mordecai's rejection, nor could it wait until the month of Adar arrived to gain satisfaction.

On advice from his wife and friends, Haman had a gallows built. On this, he hoped to hang

Xerxes offered Esther "up to half the kingdom" (5:3, 6). We must always be careful about what we say to others, making sure that we can fulfill our promises. Herodotus wrote that another woman once responded to Xerxes' generous offer by requesting a beautiful robe that had been given to the king by Queen Amestris. The fallout from that incident was extremely unfavorable. Do not make promises without first anticipating the consequences.

Haman's hatred of Mordecai had grown so intense that it destroyed any satisfaction Haman could have found in his own activities. Hatred grows into bitterness with disastrous changes in the person who hates. Heed well the warning of Hebrews: "See to it . . . that no bitter root grows up to cause trouble and defile many" (Heb. 12:15).

Zeresh

Haman's wife, Zeresh, also served as his counselor, advising him on what to do with Mordecai. Her advice partly brought about Haman's tragic fall. Various suggestions have been offered concerning the meaning of the name *Zeresh.* One colorful proposal is "shaggy head," referring to someone with disheveled hair.

Mordecai. The height of these gallows is reported to be fifty cubits, equivalent to seventy-five feet (5:14), which could be an exaggeration to emphasize a structure built much larger than needed. On the other hand, the measurement might include a hill upon which the gallows were built. Haman certainly would want to make a display of Mordecai's punishment to show the community who had ultimately won in the contest of wills.

Haman's mood at this point is described by the word *delighted* (5:14), but that mood would not last. The story of Esther now moved to the theme of reversal. The fortunes of the Jewish people were about to be reversed. The outcome of events would be reversed, as would the fates of the story's leading characters as well.

- All of the Jews, including Mordecai, were
- scheduled for annihilation in the month of
- Adar. Yet Haman simply could not wait until
- then. Human pride leads people to commit
- rash actions, and such actions often have
- drastic consequences.

QUESTIONS TO GUIDE YOUR STUDY

1. Why does God choose to act "through" the efforts of His people rather than just acting by Himself on their behalf?

2. How do hatred and envy tend to blind us to the good things of life that are part of our everyday experiences? Why is it important to "put aside" past hurts and move on?

3. In what ways were Haman's family and friends as self-centered as he?

The fourth section of the book of Esther (6:1–7:10) features the key reversal in Haman's and Mordecai's fates. Mordecai was honored by the king, much to Haman's humiliation (Esther 6). The final indignation of foolish Haman was his pathetic effort to save himself from the gallows which he himself had ordered constructed (Esther 7).

HAMAN MUST HONOR MORDECAI (6:1–14)

Haman was tricked into planning a ceremony to honor Mordecai, his enemy. Human intrigue, manipulation, and simple coincidence are the overt explanations for the dramatic changes in the story's direction. Yet behind the surprising turn of events was God, covertly at work.

The King's Sleepless Night (6:1–3)

The reason for the king's insomnia is not stated, but the details of the story point to God's providence. The fate of thousands of Jews pivoted on this episode. Up to this point, a great injustice had been looming as the calendar moved toward the execution of the king's decree in Adar. Now God's hand was felt, preserving His people. It was not merely coincidence that Xerxes could not sleep on "that night" (6:1). It was the night before: On the approaching day, Esther would host her second banquet and make known her request, and Haman would seek the king's permission to hang Mordecai.

To pass the sleepless night, the king had his servants read the royal annals. These were probably the official court records that were compiled as a history of each king's reign. Such a massive amount of material could not be read in one night, so the servants selected a portion for reading on this particular night. Again, it was not just coincidence that the selection included the account of how Mordecai saved the king (2:21–23).

Heroes who performed worthy deeds on behalf of Persian kings were usually honored or rewarded in some manner. Sleeplessness and a chronicle reading led the king to realize that Mordecai had never been honored for his role in protecting him. That oversight had to be corrected.

N

■ *Relief comes to God's faithful people from*
■ *unexpected sources and at opportune*
■ *moments. Why should we be surprised when*
■ *God acts on our behalf at just the right time?*

Cyrus and Xerxes

Xerxes probably did not realize that his hearing of a particular reading from the chronicles was not coincidence; God was involved. An earlier Persian king had a similar experience. Cyrus the Great, who ruled from about 550 to 530 B.C., freed the captives Babylon had taken during its harsh rule. They were allowed to return to rebuild the city of Jerusalem and its Temple. Cyrus is referred to as the Lord's shepherd and anointed one (Isa. 44:28—45:1).

Haman Devises Mordecai's Honor (6:4–9)

The theme of reversed expectations is first realized in Haman's mind. Imagine his excited thoughts as he approached the king's palace, probably very early the next morning. Before this day was done, he thought he would dine with the king and queen and, perhaps more satisfying, he would have Mordecai the Jew executed.

Haman's expectations were high as he entered the palace court, but he had no chance to follow through. Once in Xerxes's presence, he was consulted immediately on how the king should honor someone. Due to his corrupted ego, Haman assumed the king must intend to honor him—who else was so worthy? Haman's expectations for the day rose to new heights as he invented a pompous program of accolade.

Ironically, Haman's egotism caused him unintentionally to devise a magnificent ceremony to honor Mordecai (6:7–9). Imagining himself as the recipient, Haman chose the highest honors: to be dressed in the king's royal robes; to ride on the king's royal horse (on royal saddlery); and to have heralds proclaiming official praises. However, Haman was about to learn that he would not be the person enjoying these honors.

Haman thought that no one besides himself was worthy of the king's highest honor. He should have known one of Israel's wisdom sayings: "Pride goes before destruction, a haughty spirit before a fall" (Prov. 16:18).

- *Haman was tricked into planning an elabo-*
- *rate ceremony to honor Mordecai. The trick-*
- *ery, however, was not planned by the king.*
- *Rather, Haman's own pride and arrogance*
- *prevented him from considering people*
- *besides himself as worthy of praise.*

Haman Is Humbled Before Mordecai (6:10–11)

Haman was excited to hear Xerxes say, "Do just as you have suggested" (6:10). He thought the king was agreeing to honor him in such a grandiose manner. But how shocked he was to hear the king finish his instructions with "for Mordecai the Jew"!

Xerxes showed himself again as a king who did not have full knowledge of events in his own kingdom. He knew that Mordecai was a Jew and that he had granted Haman authority to destroy a "disobedient" people. He was not aware that the Jews, including Mordecai, were the people Haman sought to annihilate.

The depiction of Mordecai dressed in royalty and being led on horseback by Haman (6:11) anticipates their inverted roles to come. Haman's expectations had already changed

How fast Haman's life changed! One day he boasted about being "the only person Queen Esther invited to accompany the king" (Esther 5:12), and the next day his downfall had already begun. Since we do not know what might happen tomorrow, why should we boast about what we will do in the future? Only God really knows (James 4:13–16).

dramatically. He began the morning expecting to hang Mordecai and exalt himself. Instead, he was exalting Mordecai and humiliating himself before all those who knew of his hatred for this Jew.

A Different Outlook (6:12–14)

After such humiliation, Haman returned home in grief, covering his head as was the practice of people mourning some great tragedy. When Mordecai's rejection had upset Haman on an earlier occasion, he found solace among his family and friends. This time they could not comfort him; indeed, they saw that matters were only going to get worse.

Haman's advisors as well as his wife warned that Mordecai's "Jewish origin" (6:13) spelled eventual ruin for Haman. The king, who had chosen to honor this particular Jew, would soon discover that the Jews were the people Haman had plotted to destroy. If, in addition, Xerxes learned of the gallows constructed to hang Mordecai, Haman's standing with the king was surely doomed.

Covering the Head

Haman used a common expression of grief when he returned home "with his head covered" (Esther 6:12). Just how he covered his head is not certain. Sadness or grief was shown by putting one's hand on the head and by putting ashes on it (2 Sam. 13:19).

The king's scheming grand vizier had been in control, even manipulating the king to adopt particular policies. Now Haman found himself out of control, as the king's eunuchs arrived to escort him to the banquet. Mordecai's exaltation surely raised Haman's anxiety level: How would the king react when he realized the Jews were decreed for destruction? What if the king asked about the gallows?

- *Life's circumstances can change so quickly.*
- *Haman ended one day boasting of his status in*
- *life and finished the next humiliated and appre-*
- *hensive of the future. Since we do not know*
- *what the future holds, we should seek God's*
- *will and not boast of our self-sufficiency.*

QUESTIONS TO GUIDE YOUR STUDY

1. List several "good" events of your life that appear to be coincidental. How many of these events could have resulted from God working silently in your life?

2. Mordecai did not receive his reward for saving the king until some time after the incident. How can we learn to be patient and wait on God's timing for our earthly rewards?

3. Relatives and personal friends should help us face our faults and improve ourselves. In what ways did Haman's wife and friends contribute more to his downfall than they did to his betterment?

The reversal of the fates of Mordecai and Haman took place quickly. Not only did Mordecai get the best of Haman, but Esther outsmarted him as well.

HAMAN'S HANGING (7:1–10)

Feasting is prominent in the book of Esther. Xerxes' seven-day feast at the beginning of the story ultimately resulted in Esther's appointment as queen. Queen Esther's two banquets resulted in the condemnation of the Jew's enemy—Haman.

Esther's Second Banquet (7:1–2)

On the following day, Esther assembled her guests for the second banquet, during which she would reveal her entreaty as she had promised (5:7–8). While dining, Haman must have been agitated by the day's events. What would his enemy Mordecai do with his new popularity? How would the king react to the Jews' scheduled destruction?

When Haman focused on the banquet, he noticed how committed the king was to Esther. Xerxes immediately inquired about Esther's petition, again offering her "up to half the kingdom" (7:2). It was clear to Haman that because of Esther's favor with the king, she would be granted whatever she desired.

Once a powerful Haman had sat drinking with the king while the Jews were powerless (3:15). Now the flow of power had been reversed, and the story emphasizes Esther's advantage by repeatedly addressing her as "Queen Esther" throughout chapter 7.

The Banquet Hall

The feast that Esther prepared for Haman and the king was an elaborate meal, combined with the drinking of wine (Esther 7:2). Banquets were usually held in the evening and, especially in the case of a royal affair, served in rooms specially constructed for such occasions. Since wine was an important part of the feast, the Hebrew expression for the banquet hall is "house of the feast of wine."

Esther Makes Her Request (7:3–7)

Esther alluded to Haman's plot to destroy her people, herself included. She did not mention the Jews by name, but Haman knew exactly what she meant. She spoke of being "sold for destruction and slaughter and annihilation" (7:4), so the king would be fully aware of the decree Haman had put in place.

Throughout the book of Esther, Xerxes had been uninformed about major events in his kingdom. Now he was bewildered that his queen's life was threatened and perplexed about who was responsible. Esther may have feared the influence that Haman, as grand vizier, would have with the king. Nevertheless, she did not hesitate to identify Haman as her adversary (7:6).

Reactions to Esther's revelation were swift. The king realized that Haman had maneuvered him into establishing a royal decree that would take the life of his beloved queen. Haman realized that he was powerless and doomed.

The Dining Couch

Banquets and feasts were prominent in sealing friendships, celebrating victories, and sharing joyous occasions. In oriental societies, banqueters assumed positions unfamiliar to westerners. Those who dined reclined on bedlike seats and lay at right angles to the table. When Haman begged Queen Esther for his life at the banquet, he approached the dining couch where she was reclining for the meal (Esther 7:8).

- *Rulers seek power through political posturing, deception, and betrayal. Esther found true power in the virtues of loyalty, honesty, and fasting in worship of God.*

Haman Is Condemned (7:8–10)

Esther's intervention had unmasked Haman's scheme, and even this egotistical villain knew that power now resided with the queen. He begged for her mercy, thus violating protocol with the king's harem. Haman's situation was already serious, but he magnified his folly by stumbling to Esther's couch, creating the appearance of impropriety.

Haman's doom was sealed with the irate king. The "word" that left the king's mouth (7:8) probably refers to a command from Xerxes, not reported in the story, to execute Haman.

We do not know if a method of execution was determined at the moment Haman's face was covered (7:8). But immediately one of the king's eunuchs announced the gallows that stood at Haman's house. Reacting emotionally, Xerxes ordered Haman to be hanged on the very gallows he had designed for Mordecai the Jew.

Haman could not rest until he rid himself of "that Jew Mordecai." Hatred led to evil scheming, which ultimately resulted in Haman's own downfall. When evildoers seem to be thriving, we should remember that their end has been predicted (Prov. 29:16).

QUESTIONS TO GUIDE YOUR STUDY

1. Of what crucial circumstance was Haman not aware while he was masterminding his scheme?

2. King Xerxes was enraged to learn that Haman's plot endangered Queen Esther. In what way was Xerxes himself responsible for the situation?

3. Haman begged Esther for his life, but could Esther have saved him even if she wanted to?

ESTHER 8

The fifth section of the book of Esther (8:1–9:32) continues the theme of reversal. Mordecai wrote a royal decree which would reverse Haman's evil decree by canceling its effect (Esther 8). The day on which the Jews were scheduled for destruction became a day of triumph and celebration (Esther 9).

THE KING'S DECREE ON THE JEWS' BEHALF (8:1–17)

Haman was now gone, but his edict to annihilate the Jews was still in effect and could not be revoked. King Xerxes, who had authorized Haman to write the first decree, now authorized Esther and Mordecai to write a second (8:8). Their decree enabled the Jews to fight against their enemies.

Esther and Mordecai Are Rewarded (8:1–2)

Part of Haman's evil plan had been to "plunder the goods" of his Jewish victims (3:13). But the reversal of his personal fate affected his property as well. Rather than Jewish property falling into Haman's hands, Haman's property was given to Esther.

Haman's authority was now assumed by Mordecai. The king's signet ring, which Haman had worn, was placed on Mordecai's hand, and Esther assigned Haman's estate to her cousin. Haman's wife and friends now found themselves under the control of the very man they had recommended for the gallows (5:14).

Xerxes executed Haman and gave his estate to Queen Esther. The historian Herodotus indicated that the practice of seizing the property of a condemned criminal was customary in the Persian Empire.

Apparently, the same custom was followed in Israel. After Queen Jezebel had the vineyard owner Naboth falsely condemned and executed, she advised her husband, King Ahab, to take possession of Naboth's property (1 Kings 21:7–16).

The signet ring that had been on Haman's hand was now on Mordecai's. An Israelite wisdom saying was played out in the separate fates of these two men: "The righteousness of the upright delivers them, but the unfaithful are trapped by evil desires" (Prov. 11:6).

SN

■ God's providence brought rewards to Esther
■ and Mordecai for their faithfulness and will-
■ ingness to risk their own security in order to
■ save others. Rewards often result from faith-
■ ful service to God, but they are not guaran-
■ teed and should not be the motive for our
■ actions.

Esther Pleads for Her People (8:3–6)

The reversal of power and fortune from Haman to Esther and Mordecai was complete. But Haman's villainous plot remained, so Esther pleaded for the king's assistance to avert the disaster. If Mordecai was right to suggest that Esther may have become queen for the express purpose of saving her people (4:14), she was now fulfilling that purpose.

The King's New Decree (8:7–8)

Xerxes regretted authorizing Haman to write a royal decree that not even the king could revoke. To reassure Esther that he opposed the effort to destroy the Jews, Xerxes reminded her how he had hanged Haman and turned over his estate to the queen.

Since Haman's decree was irrevocable, Xerxes instructed Esther and Mordecai to write a counter decree. This decree would also carry the king's name and be sealed with the king's signet ring, but it would favor the Jews.

N

- *Each interaction between Esther and Xerxes*
- *demonstrates that the queen had won the*
- *king's heart. Esther's great favor with Xerxes*
- *was certainly one of her strengths. While*
- *Haman shows us how to use personal influ-*
- *ence for self-centered and harmful purposes,*
- *Esther shows us how to do it righteously for*
- *the good of others.*

Countering Haman's Decree (8:9–14)

Two months and ten days passed between the month of Nisan, when Haman's decree had been published (3:12–14), and the month of Sivan (8:9). Mordecai made use of the same royal resources Haman had used against the Jews. Royal secretaries wrote the orders, and mounted couriers published them throughout the provinces of the empire.

Mordecai's decree gave the Jews the right to defend themselves. The same actions authorized by Haman against the Jews—to destroy, kill, annihilate, and plunder—were by this new decree granted to them. An important stipulation restricted the Jews to fighting only those who "might attack them" (8:11). Mordecai was authorizing self-defense, not aggression.

The Jews Rejoice (8:15–17)

Fortunes had changed for the Jews. One of their own had been promoted to Haman's position, second to the king. To see Mordecai dressed in royal attire must have brought joy (8:15). But Mordecai's decree gladdened their hearts even more.

The reversal of decrees resulted in a reversal of mood in the city of Susa. Whereas Haman's

The Signet Ring

The king's signet was his seal, usually in the form of a ring with the seal carefully crafted upon it. Using the signet ring, an important or rich person would authenticate a document. It served much the same purpose as a signature on a document today.

Proselytes

Proselytes were non-Jews who accepted the Jewish faith and completed the rituals to become Jews. After Mordecai's decree was dispatched, "many people of other nationalities became Jews" (Esther 8:17). While these proselytes were reacting to the dramatic turn of events in Persia, others found the concept of one God creating, sustaining, and ruling all things to be superior to polytheistic views.

decree had left the city disturbed and bewildered (3:15), Mordecai's decree resulted in "joyous celebration" (8:15). Everyone sensed that a great wrong had been made right.

- ■ *The decrees of Haman and Mordecai were*
- ■ *copied and "issued as law" (3:14; 8:13). In*
- ■ *their celebrations, the Jewish people could*
- ■ *praise God for working through the normal*
- ■ *channels of government to bring about their*
- ■ *salvation.*

QUESTIONS TO GUIDE YOUR STUDY

1. Once Esther's own safety was no longer threatened, she sought deliverance for her people. How did Esther persuade the king by making her plea a personal request?

2. The story does not tell what became of Zeresh, Haman's wife. Do you suppose she had to pay for her part in advising that gallows be built for Mordecai?

3. Can you cite examples of laws in your society that, like Haman's decree, are not "good laws"? What should be the Christian's response when public leaders legislate laws that will bring harm to certain people within the society?

The theme of reversal was played out again on the thirteenth of Adar, the day planned for the Jews' destruction. This day was exchanged for the two-day celebration of Purim.

MORDECAI'S DEFENSE SAVES THE JEWS (9:1–17)

The casting of the lot (known as the *pur;* see p. 67) had indicated Adar as the month for a momentous event (3:7), so Haman had appointed that time for his plot. But when the month and day arrived, the Jews defeated their enemies.

The Jews Unite in Defense (9:1–4)

The Persian Empire was filled with anxious anticipation during the month of Adar. The thirteenth day was the appointed day for execution of two opposing royal decrees; if both were carried out, there would be much bloodshed.

Haman was dead, but while he was alive he had planted evil seeds that were ready to sprout. Despite the positions of power held by Esther and Mordecai, enemies of the Jews still were preparing to execute Haman's decree. These enemies would have included Haman's ten sons and probably many others who had been his friends and advisors.

The theme of reversal is stated simply: "Now the tables were turned" (9:1). The enemies found no support among other nations in the Persian Empire; these nations feared the Jews and would not join an attack on them. Furthermore, Mordecai's position in Xerxes's court influenced the local magistrates of the provinces to help the Jews rather than their enemies.

The Persians had cast the *pur*, selecting Adar as the month for significant events (Esther 3:7). As they cast the lots, they did not realize what the writer of Proverbs understood: "The lot is cast into the lap, but its every decision is from the LORD" (Prov. 16:33).

The political landscape in Persia had changed quickly. Those whose priority was to protect their own positions tracked the direction of power, trying to keep themselves on the winning side. Thus, the local politicians of Persia fell in behind the new man in power.

Conflict in the City (9:5–15)

Violence and bloodshed broke out on the thirteenth day. To understand what actually took place, we must review what the two decrees stipulated. Haman's decree ordered the enemies to kill, destroy, annihilate, and plunder the Jews. Mordecai's degree allowed the Jews to do the same to those who attacked them. If no enemies had attacked, the Jews would have killed no one.

The report that the Jews "did what they pleased" (9:5) expresses another reversal. The king had given Haman full authority, commenting, "Do with the people as you please" (3:11). But on the appointed day, the Jews—not Haman—were the ones doing as they pleased.

Actually, all that pleased the Jews was to defend themselves. Doing this meant fighting the enemies who attacked them. Wanting only to preserve their own lives, they chose not to plunder their enemies' goods (9:10, 15). The goal was survival, not material gain.

The thirteenth day (9:5–13). On the day that the two decrees took effect, the Jews killed five hundred of their enemies, as well as Haman's ten sons, who are listed by name (9:7–10). Although this report may make the Jews appear

During the days of oppressive persecution, the survival of the Jewish people depended upon them doing something. They could not sit back, waiting for Adar to arrive. Esther and Mordecai contributed as leaders, but the people themselves had to be involved in their own salvation—they had to defend themselves. The axiom "the Lord helps those who help themselves" was true of their situation, and it is also true of ours. After we pray, we must take action.

bloodthirsty, they actually fought only against enemies who "hated them" (9:5) and initiated attacks upon them. Furthermore, the number five hundred was only a small portion of the total population of Susa. The movement to destroy the Jews had fizzled.

At the end of the day, the king reviewed with Esther the day's events and inquired whether she thought any further action was needed. Her answer may seem cruel to us today: She requested a second day of retaliation and the public hanging of Haman's dead sons.

The fourteenth day (9:14–15). The king granted a second day, and three hundred more of their enemies were killed. Was Esther cruel or perhaps bloodthirsty herself? Both of her requests may have been a desire to save her people from destruction. The queen probably suspected that the enemies would not cease their attacks, despite the passing of the appointed day and their high losses. The Jews would be forced to fight one more day.

The hanging of the corpses of Haman's sons was a public display, following a common tactic of ancient battle used to weaken the enemies' morale. Perhaps the sight of their dead leaders would cause the enemies to stop their attacks.

Conflict in the Provinces (9:16–17)

Among all of the provinces, the Jews killed seventy-five thousand of their enemies. All the fighting in the provinces took place on the thirteenth day, since the second day of retaliation was carried out in Susa only. On the fourteenth day, the Jews in the provinces feasted and celebrated their victory, even though fighting continued in Susa.

Thousand or Clan?

The report that the Jews killed seventy-five thousand enemies is stunning. Since the Greek Old Testament reports only fifteen thousand killed, we wonder just how numerous their enemies really were.

Yet another figure can be calculated by translating the Hebrew verse differently. The Hebrew word translated "thousand" also can mean "clan." If the slain enemies numbered 75 clans, their total would have been around 3,800. Regardless of the actual figure, God had preserved His people in a great day of deliverance.

■ *Instead of being exterminated, the Jews tri-*
■ *umphed over their enemies. They fought res-*
■ *olutely, not motivated by economic factors,*
■ *but by a just cause—defending their right to*
■ *live. How tragic it is that they were forced to*
■ *choose between killing their enemies or being*
■ *massacred themselves.*

THE FEAST OF PURIM (9:18–32)

Purim commemorates the deliverance of the Jews from genocide, recalling especially the efforts of Esther and Mordecai. The story tells how the Feast of Purim was inaugurated; how it was to be celebrated; and why it was observed on certain days of the year.

The Time to Celebrate (9:18–19)

Purim is celebrated on both the fourteenth and fifteenth days of Adar. The story explains why this is so from the viewpoint of Jews dwelling in the citadel of Susa. Because they assembled in Susa to fight on two days, they did not feast until the fifteenth of Adar. Jews in the provinces, however, only fought on one day, and thus feasted a day earlier, on the fourteenth of Adar.

Mordecai's Decree (9:20–22)

Acting from his new position in the empire, Mordecai gave the official decree establishing Purim. The festival was founded by setting the fourteenth and fifteenth days of Adar as an annual time for feasting, sharing of food gifts, and giving to the poor. Whether Mordecai recorded these instructions somewhere besides in his letters to the Jews, perhaps in the royal annals, is not known.

Purim Today

Mordecai stipulated that Purim be celebrated annually. Jews today still observe the feast. Purim is celebrated on the fourteenth day of Adar, although in some places the fifteenth day is observed as "Shushan Purim." On the day preceding Purim, the thirteenth day, Jewish tradition observes the Fast of Esther to commemorate the fasting of the Jews as they sought God for deliverance.

- *The first celebrations in Susa and the prov-*
- *inces were natural responses of joy for God's*
- *deliverance. We naturally praise and thank*
- *God when we have just experienced His care.*
- *Yet we also need regular and annual celebra-*
- *tions and holidays on which we recall God's*
- *past acts on our behalf. Christmas is the most*
- *significant such time, remembering the send-*
- *ing of the Christ Child.*

The Background of the Festival (9:23–28)

With the passing of time, participants in a yearly festival sometimes forget the origin of the celebration. The story provides a reminder of Purim's origin by summarizing the events behind it. The feast was named "Purim" because of the *pur* cast by Haman (*pur* coming from a Babylonian word meaning "to cast lots"). The purpose of the feast was to memorialize Haman's wicked plot, which returned "onto his own head" (9:25).

Purim would become a community event and a tradition of the Jews based on "what had happened to them" (9:26). Mordecai's letter called for the feast to be observed by Jews and Gentiles for generations to come.

Purim and Mordecai

In the apocryphal book of 2 Maccabees, the fourteenth day of Adar is called "Mordecai's day" (2 Macc. 15:36). During the many years of celebrating Purim, the participants remembered Esther's cousin, commemorating his role in establishing the yearly feast.

- *The invitation to participate in Purim is*
- *extended not only to Jews, but also to "all*
- *who join them" (9:27). All peoples can*
- *praise God and celebrate with joy His acts*
- *of salvation.*

The Queen Confirms Purim (9:29–32)

To promote the Feast of Purim, Esther added her authority to Mordecai's instructions. Mordecai had advanced to a prominent position in the empire (9:4); nevertheless, Esther made certain that his letters outlining how and why Purim should be observed would be accepted by Jews everywhere. She endorsed Purim with her "full authority" (9:29) as queen of Persia.

QUESTIONS TO GUIDE YOUR STUDY

1. The loss of human life through war and violence is always tragic and to be avoided whenever possible. Why is self defense sometimes a justifiable reason to engage in war or fighting?

2. In what activities did the people involve themselves on the days of Purim? Why were these activities appropriate for remembering God's deliverance?

3. What are the significant religious holidays that Christians celebrate today? What acts of God do these holidays help Christians remember and relive?

A Chronology of Esther

THE DATE	THE EVENT	SCRIPTURE
Xerxes' third year (483 B.C.)	Xerxes gives a banquet for nobles and officials.	Esther 1:3
Xerxes' third year, seven days later	Vashti refuses the king's invitation and is deposed.	Esther 1:10, 12, 19
Xerxes' seventh year, the tenth month (Tebeth, 479 B.C.)	Xerxes selects Esther to be his new queen.	Esther 2:16–17
Xerxes' twelfth year, the first month (Nisan, 474 B.C.)	The Persians cast the *pur,* selecting the twelfth month, Adar. Haman's decree sets the thirteenth day of Adar for destroying the Jewish people.	Esther 3:7, 13
Xerxes' twelfth year, the third month, the twenty-third day (Sivan, 474 B.C.)	Mordecai issues a decree in the king's name on behalf of the Jews.	Esther 8:9–10
Xerxes' twelfth year, the twelfth month, the thirteenth day (Adar, 474 B.C.)	The Jews kill 500 enemies in Susa and 75,000 enemies in the provinces.	Esther 9:1, 6, 16
Xerxes' twelfth year, the twelfth month, the fourteenth day (Adar, 474 B.C.)	The Jews kill 300 more enemies in Susa. Jews in the provinces celebrate a day of feasting.	Esther 9:15, 17
Xerxes' twelfth year, the twelfth month, the fifteenth day (Adar, 474 B.C.)	The Jews in Susa celebrate a day of feasting.	Esther 9:18

ESTHER 10

The Distant Shores

The expression "distant shores" (Esther 10:1) reflects the expanse of Xerxes's empire. The greatest extension of the Persian Empire came under Xerxes's father Darius I. Under Darius, Persia became a vast collection of states and kingdoms reaching from the Indus River Valley in the east to the shores of Asia Minor in the west. It reached northward to southern Russia, and in the south included Egypt and the regions bordering the Persian Gulf and the Gulf of Oman.

Persian expansion was stalled when Darius attempted to conquer the Greeks but was unsuccessful. He lost to the Greeks at Marathon in 490 B.C. Later kings, including Xerxes, did little to expand the empire, and they even had difficulty holding such a far-flung empire together.

The final section of the book of Esther (10:1–3) forms a brief epilogue to the story.

MORDECAI'S PROMOTION (10:1–3)

The story concludes the way it began by describing the power and influence of Xerxes in his great kingdom. The magnificent Xerxes "who ruled over 127 provinces" (1:1) was powerful enough to tax peoples throughout his empire, even to its distant shores (probably of the Mediterranean Sea).

The theme of reversal is developed one last time. In the first section of the story, Queen Vashti was demoted; in the last section, Mordecai was promoted. Early in the story Haman, the Jews' enemy, was promoted over "all the other nobles" (3:1). Now Mordecai was made "second in rank" to the king.

The differences between Haman and Mordecai become evident by reflecting on Mordecai's greatness. The high esteem which Mordecai enjoyed was well earned, for he "worked for the good of his people" (10:3). Haman, however, had worked for his own personal good, being most concerned about the honor and praise he thought he should receive.

Mordecai the Jew contributed to the prosperity of the Persian Empire. Through his efforts, the Jews were vindicated as a people. If Haman had succeeded in his efforts, the Persian Empire would have lost an entire segment of its population in a gruesome bloodbath. Instead, thanks to Mordecai's rise, the empire enjoyed peace.

- When Xerxes gave a banquet for his military
- leaders, nobles, and princes the first time,
- Mordecai was an unknown Jew in the king-
- dom. Now a "full account" of Mordecai's
- accomplishments were recorded in the royal
- annals. His name would be at the top of the
- guest list for the king's next banquet.

QUESTIONS TO GUIDE YOUR STUDY

1. What godly traits does Mordecai exem-
plify? What could leaders today learn
from his use of power?
2. What similarities do you see between
Joseph in Egypt, Daniel in Babylon, and
Mordecai in Persia?

The following list is a collection of source works that will provide either more specific information on the books of Ruth and Esther or an expanded treatment of themes and topics related to these books.

Breneman, Mervin. *Ezra, Nehemiah, Esther* (The New American Commentary), vol. 10. A more scholarly treatment of the text of Esther that provides emphases on the text itself, background, and theological considerations.

Holman Bible Dictionary. An exhaustive, alphabetically arranged resource of Bible-related subjects. An excellent tool of definitions and other infomation on the people, places, things, and events of the Bible.

Holman Bible Handbook. A comprehensive treatment of Ruth and Esther that offers outlines, commentary on key themes and sections, and full-color photos, illustrations, charts, and maps. Provides an emphasis on the broader theological messages of Ruth and Esther.

Kent, Dan G., *Joshua, Judges, Ruth* (Layman's Bible Book Commentary). A popular-level treatment of the book of Ruth. This easy-to-use volume provides a relevant and practical perspective.

NIV Disciple's Study Bible. A study Bible offering over 10,000 annotations on the Bible. A valuable resource for relating the messages of Ruth and Esther to the key doctrines of the Christian faith. Provides a theological introduction to each book of the Bible, as well as insights for putting faith into practice.

Owens, Mary Frances. *Ezra, Nehemiah, Esther, Job* (Layman's Bible Book Commentary). A popular-level treatment of the book of Esther. This easy-to-use volume provides a relevant and practical perspective on the events of Esther.